The Retirement Planning Accelerator

The Fast-Track Guide to Financial Independence, Healthcare Planning, Optimized Tax Strategies, and a Secure Future

Jon J. McKenzie

Published by
Parkwood Publishing

DEDICATION

Stacy,

My rock, my best friend, my everything.

This book is as much yours as it is mine, for I could never have achieved this without your unwavering support, your endless patience, and your boundless love. I am forever grateful for the support and encouragement you've given me.

You believed in me even when I doubted myself, and for that, I am eternally thankful.

"2 Hearts 1 Love"

With all my love,
Jon

© Copyright Jon J. McKenzie, 2024 - All rights reserved.

The content within this book may not be reproduced, duplicated or transmitted without direct written permission from the author or the publisher.

Under no circumstances will any blame or legal responsibility be held against the publisher, or author, for any damages, reparation, or monetary loss due to the information contained within this book. Either directly or indirectly. You are responsible for your own choices, actions, and results.

Legal Notice:

This book is copyright protected. This book is only for personal use. You cannot amend, distribute, sell, use, quote or paraphrase any part, of the content within this book, without the consent of the author or publisher.

Disclaimer Notice:

Please note the information contained within this document is for educational and entertainment purposes only. All effort has been expended to present accurate, up-to-date, and reliable, complete information. No warranties of any kind are declared or implied. Readers acknowledge that the author is not engaging in the rendering of legal, financial, medical or professional advice. The content within this book has been derived from various sources. Please consult a licensed professional before attempting any techniques outlined in this book.

By reading this document, the reader agrees that under no circumstances is the author responsible for any losses, direct or indirect, which are incurred as a result of the use of the information contained within this document, including, but not limited to, — errors, omissions, or inaccuracies.

TABLE OF CONTENTS

Introduction 1

Chapter 1: Understanding Your Financial Foundation 4

Chapter 2: Investment Strategies for Different Life Stages 14

Chapter 3: Navigating Healthcare Costs and Planning 26

Chapter 4: Optimizing Tax Strategies for Retirement 35

Chapter 5: Deciding Your Ideal Retirement Age 45

Chapter 6: Creating a Sustainable Retirement Income Plan 55

Chapter 7: Estate Planning and Legacy Building 67

Chapter 8: Real Estate Investing for Retirement 77

Chapter 9: Addressing Common Retirement Fears and Misconceptions 87

Chapter 10: Embracing a Holistic Retirement Lifestyle 98

Chapter 11: Future-Proofing Your Retirement Plan 108

Conclusion 122

References 124

INTRODUCTION

Retirement planning often feels like a distant worry until suddenly it isn't. Did you know nearly half of Americans saved less than $10,000 for retirement? This startling fact underscores a looming crisis. Many need to prepare for the financial demands of their golden years. The urgency of planning becomes clear when we recognize that living longer means we need more money to sustain our lifestyles.

The purpose of this book is straightforward. I want to change how you view retirement planning. It's not a burdensome task but an exciting opportunity to secure your future. By approaching retirement with the right mindset, you can turn a daunting challenge into a rewarding journey. This book guides you in transforming fear into confidence through strategic planning and informed decision-making.

Let me share a bit about myself. My journey began in the kitchen as a chef, where I learned the importance of precision and timing. These skills served me well as I transitioned into entrepreneurship, founding multiple successful businesses. My passion lies in financial empowerment, and I am committed to helping you achieve financial independence. I understand the grit required to succeed in any field, and I bring that same determination to guide you toward a secure retirement.

This book is structured to cover all the critical components of retirement planning. We will explore financial independence, effective healthcare strategies, optimized tax planning, and estate management. Each chapter builds on the last, offering a comprehensive toolkit to design your financial future. This structure ensures you receive a well-rounded guide to creating lasting wealth and security.

I know the challenges you face. Many of you need more savings. Others feel overwhelmed by investment decisions or anxious about rising healthcare costs. These concerns are valid, and you are not alone. Research shows that these are common hurdles for many planning their retirements. I aim to address these pain points with empathy and understanding. Together, we will confront these challenges head-on.

Expect practical solutions. This book is filled with actionable strategies and exercises designed to empower you. You will find tools and knowledge to overcome obstacles and take control of your retirement planning. Each chapter offers specific steps you can implement immediately, ensuring you make tangible progress toward your goals.

Throughout the book, you will encounter real-world examples and case studies. These stories illustrate key concepts and demonstrate successful strategies in action. By learning from others' experiences, you will gain insights into effective planning techniques and see the potential for success in your journey.

As you delve into these pages, I want to inspire you to take charge of your financial future. Retirement planning is not just about accumulating money. It's about creating a fulfilling and secure life for yourself and your loved ones. You have the power to shape your destiny, and this book is here to guide you every step of the way.

So, let's start this journey together. You can transform your future into financial independence and peace of mind with the proper knowledge and tools. The path to a secure retirement is at your fingertips. Let's begin.

Henry Ford – "Whether you think you can, or you think you can't – you're right."

CHAPTER 1: UNDERSTANDING YOUR FINANCIAL FOUNDATION

Consider a couple in their early fifties who struggled to piece together their financial puzzle despite earning a comfortable income. They had assets, but they also had debts, and their savings were less robust than they hoped. Like many, they were caught in the whirlwind of daily life, rarely pausing to assess where they stood financially. This situation is common; many individuals must clearly understand their financial health before they drift through their prime earning years. This chapter is your starting point, a comprehensive guide to assessing your financial position, identifying strengths and weaknesses, and setting achievable goals. It's about gaining clarity to build a solid foundation for your future.

1.1 Assessing Your Current Financial Health

Conducting a thorough financial audit is essential to understanding your financial health. Start by calculating your net worth. Firstly, list all your assets—such as your home, vehicles, investment accounts, and any other valuable property—and subtract your liabilities, like mortgages, car loans, and credit card debt. The resulting figure provides a snapshot of your overall financial position. Next, analyze your monthly cash flow. Track your income sources and all expenses, from fixed costs like rent or mortgage payments to variable expenses such as groceries and entertainment. This analysis will help you understand where your money goes each month and identify areas where you can cut back. Inventory your assets and liabilities to clarify what you own and owe, including everything from savings accounts and 401(k) balances to outstanding loans and credit card debt. Finally, assess your current savings and investment portfolio. Determine if your savings align with your retirement goals and if your investments align with your risk tolerance and time horizon.

Identifying your financial strengths and weaknesses allows you to focus on areas needing improvement. Start by pinpointing high-interest debts, which can quickly erode your wealth. These often include high rates for credit card balances and personal loans. Evaluate your spending habits to uncover unnecessary expenses. Some examples of such expenses can be frequent dining out, subscription services you no longer use, or impulse purchases. Assess your existing emergency fund to ensure it's sufficient to cover unexpected expenses, like medical emergencies or car repairs. An adequate emergency fund should cover three to six months' worth of living expenses, providing a financial cushion in times of need.

Establishing financial goals is critical for long-term success. Use the SMART goal-setting framework to create specific, measurable, achievable, relevant, and time-bound objectives. Start with short-term goals, such as paying off a particular debt or increasing your savings rate by a certain percentage within the next six months. Then, outline long-term goals, like saving for a child's education or planning for retirement. Prioritize these financial objectives based on urgency and importance, ensuring you focus on what matters most. For example, paying down high-interest debt may take precedence over building a vacation fund if it significantly impacts your financial health.

Utilize Financial Tools and Resources

To assist in ongoing assessment, leverage personal finance software. Apps like Simplifi or Quicken Classic can help you track spending, manage budgets, and visualize your financial health. These tools provide insights into your spending patterns and help you make informed decisions. Additionally, consider consulting a financial planner. A professional can offer personalized advice and strategies tailored to your unique situation, helping you optimize your financial plan. They can also assist in navigating complex financial decisions, such as investment choices or tax strategies, providing peace of mind as you work toward your goals.

By systematically reviewing your financial status, you understand where you stand and what steps you need to take to improve your financial health. This foundational knowledge empowers you to make informed decisions and set a course toward a secure and prosperous future.

1.2 Creating a Personalized Savings Blueprint

Savings are the bedrock of financial security and retirement planning. Without them, any unexpected expense can quickly derail your financial stability. Think of your savings as a safety net that catches you when life throws a curveball and enables long-term economic independence. Consider an emergency fund, a crucial component of your savings. It cushions against unforeseen events like medical emergencies or sudden job loss. This fund is not just a number in your bank account; it's peace of mind. Long-term savings, on the other hand, are your ticket to financial independence. They represent your ability to retire comfortably, pursue passions, and live without the constant stress of economic insecurity. By building a robust savings plan, you're laying the groundwork for a future where you're in control.

Setting savings targets can seem daunting, but breaking them down into short-term and long-term goals makes the task manageable. Short-term savings should focus on specific goals, like saving for a vacation, a new car, or even home renovations. These are goals you can achieve in one to three years. They keep you motivated and provide a sense of accomplishment as you tick them off your list. Long-term savings, however, require more foresight. These are savings for retirement, your children's education, or significant life events. Establishing these targets involves forecasting your future needs and working backward to determine how much you need to save now. It's about being realistic yet ambitious, ensuring your goals are both challenging and attainable.

Developing a customized savings plan is where the real magic happens. This plan should reflect your unique financial situation and goals. Start by automating savings contributions. Set up automatic transfers from your checking account to your savings or investment accounts. This strategy ensures consistency and reduces the temptation to spend. Next, consider creating savings buckets for different goals. Each bucket should represent a specific emergency, travel, or retirement objective. This method keeps your savings organized and purpose-driven. Adjust your savings plan as life changes. Whether you receive a raise or face an unexpected expense, your savings strategy should evolve accordingly. Flexibility is critical, allowing you to adapt while staying on track with your goals.

Regularly monitoring and adjusting your savings strategies is crucial to ensure they align with your financial goals. Conduct a quarterly savings review to assess your progress. This practice helps you identify areas where you're falling short and allows you to make necessary adjustments. If your savings are consistently below target, consider reallocating your resources. You should cut back on discretionary spending or find additional income sources. As your goals evolve, so should your savings plan. Life is dynamic, and your financial strategy should reflect that. Regular reviews keep you accountable and allow you to celebrate your successes and recalibrate when needed.

Interactive Element: Savings Goals Checklist

To assist you in this process, consider using a savings goals checklist. This simple tool can help you organize and prioritize your savings objectives, ensuring you stay focused and motivated. List your short-term and long-term goals and their target amounts and deadlines. Regularly review and update this checklist to reflect your progress and any priority changes. By keeping a tangible record of your goals, you create a visual reminder of what you're working toward, which can be incredibly motivating.

Incorporating these strategies into your financial plan will help you build a solid savings foundation. This blueprint is not just about accumulating wealth; it's about creating a life of security and opportunity. Remember, savings are not a one-time effort but an ongoing commitment to your future. With a clear plan and consistent effort, you can achieve financial independence and live the life you've always envisioned.

1.3 Balancing Debt and Savings for Retirement

The path to financial security in retirement involves more than just saving; it requires a careful balance between reducing debt and building savings. To achieve this, you must first grasp the full scope of your debt situation. Debt can be categorized into two main types: secured and unsecured. Secured debts are tied to an asset, such as a home mortgage or car loan, where the asset serves as collateral. Unsecured debts, like credit card balances or personal loans, do not have collateral backing. Knowing the types of debt you hold helps prioritize which to tackle first. High interest rates, often associated with unsecured debt, can significantly impact your financial health by increasing the total amount you owe over time. Understanding how these interest rates affect your debt can guide you in making more informed decisions about which debts to prioritize and how aggressively to pay them off.

Once you understand your debt, the next step is developing an effective debt management strategy. Two popular methods for paying down debt are the snowball and avalanche methods. The snowball method involves paying off debts from smallest to largest, gaining momentum as each balance is cleared. This approach provides quick wins, which can be motivating. In contrast, the avalanche method focuses on paying off debts with the highest interest rates first, potentially saving you more interest payments over time. Both strategies have their merits, and choosing one depends on your personal preferences and financial goals. Refinancing or consolidating debts can also be viable options, especially for high-interest obligations. By consolidating multiple debts into a single loan with a lower interest rate, you can simplify payments and reduce the total interest paid.

Balancing debt repayment with saving for retirement requires careful planning. A common challenge is determining how much income to allocate toward debt reduction versus savings. One approach is to set clear debt reduction priorities based on interest rates and balances while maintaining contributions to retirement accounts. This way, you don't sacrifice long-term financial goals while addressing immediate liabilities. Allocating income effectively might involve adjusting spending habits or increasing income through side jobs or investments. Finding a balance that doesn't compromise your retirement savings but still allows for significant progress in reducing debt is crucial.

Setting financial milestones can be a powerful motivator in managing debt and savings. Milestones act as checkpoints, helping you track progress and celebrate achievements. For example, paying off a credit card or personal loan can be a significant milestone that boosts your confidence and reinforces positive financial habits. Similarly, reaching a savings milestone, like accumulating a set percentage of your annual income in a retirement account, validates your efforts and keeps you motivated. As you reduce debt, consider reallocating the freed-up funds toward savings, accelerating your progress toward financial independence. This dynamic approach ensures that your savings potential increases as one financial burden decreases, creating a positive feedback loop.

The balancing act between managing debt and saving for retirement is a dynamic process that requires regular reassessment and adjustment. Financial circumstances change, and your strategy should evolve accordingly. The key is to remain flexible and responsive to changes in income, expenses, and life circumstances. Regularly review your financial situation to ensure that your approach to debt and savings remains aligned with your overarching financial goals. Whether adjusting to a new job, changing family dynamics, or shifting in the economic landscape, staying proactive in your financial planning will help you maintain the delicate equilibrium between debt reduction and savings growth. This balanced approach lays the foundation for a secure retirement, allowing you to enjoy your later years with financial peace of mind.

1.4 Building a Robust Emergency Fund

An emergency fund is a financial cushion and a cornerstone of financial stability. It acts as a safety net, providing immediate liquidity when life throws unexpected expenses your way. Whether it's an unforeseen medical bill, a car repair, or a temporary job loss, having a cash reserve can prevent you from spiraling into debt. This fund is readily accessible money set aside for emergencies, ensuring that other financial goals remain intact. By maintaining liquidity, you protect yourself from liquidating assets or taking out high-interest loans, which could jeopardize your financial health. Think of it as your financial insurance that offers peace of mind and the ability to navigate financial storms confidently.

Determining the right size for your emergency fund is a critical step in your financial planning. Calculate your monthly expenses, including rent or mortgage payments, utilities, groceries, transportation, healthcare, and other necessary costs. This calculation provides a baseline for understanding how much you need to sustain your lifestyle. A general guideline is multiplying your monthly expenses by three to six months to determine the appropriate size for your fund. For instance, if your monthly expenses total $3,000, aim for an emergency fund of $9,000 to $18,000. Adjust these multipliers based on your circumstances. A three-month fund may suffice if you have a stable job and minimal dependents. However, if your income is variable or you have several dependents, consider expanding your fund to cover six months or more. This strategic approach tailors your fund to your needs, ensuring it adequately supports you during unforeseen events.

Building an emergency fund requires a deliberate and consistent effort. Start by setting up automatic transfers to a dedicated savings account. This approach ensures regular contributions without relying on manual intervention, making it easier to accumulate savings over time. Even small, incremental savings can grow significantly with consistency. For example, transferring $50 every week can lead to savings of over $2,600 in a year. Consider increasing these transfers incrementally as your financial situation improves, such as after a raise or once a debt is paid off. This method allows your fund to grow alongside your financial capacity, enhancing your preparedness.

Maintaining and wisely using your emergency fund is as important as building it. Clearly define what constitutes an emergency to avoid unnecessary withdrawals. Genuine emergencies typically include unexpected medical bills, urgent home or vehicle repairs, or temporary job loss. Routine expenses or planned purchases, however, should maintain this fund. When you need to use your emergency fund, replenish it immediately. Consider temporarily increasing your savings rate or redirecting funds from non-essential expenses to rebuild your reserve. This disciplined approach ensures your fund remains robust and ready to serve its purpose whenever needed.

Ultimately, a well-established emergency fund empowers you to face life's uncertainties with resilience. It is about having money set aside and creating a financial foundation supporting your broader goals. As you continue to build and maintain this fund, you foster a sense of security and confidence that extends beyond your immediate financial needs. This proactive step in managing your finances equips you to handle unexpected challenges without compromising your financial future. With a robust emergency fund, you can pursue your aspirations knowing you have a reliable safety net to fall back on.

Elon Musk – "When something is important enough, you do it even if the odds are not in your favor."

CHAPTER 2: INVESTMENT STRATEGIES FOR DIFFERENT LIFE STAGES

Imagine standing at the base of a mountain, gazing up at its peak. The ascent may seem daunting, but reaching the summit becomes achievable with the right tools and knowledge. Investing is much like this climb. It requires preparation, understanding, and a clear path forward. For beginners, the investment landscape can appear vast and intimidating. However, with a firm grasp of basic concepts, you can start your journey toward financial growth and security. The first step is to understand the difference between stocks and bonds. Stocks represent ownership in a company and offer potential for high returns, but they come with volatility. Bonds loans to governments or corporations provide more stable returns and lower risk. Together, they form the core of most investment portfolios, balancing growth and security.

2.1 Investment Basics for Beginners

Mutual funds and exchange-traded funds (ETFs) are vital tools in the investor's toolkit. They pool money from many investors to purchase a diversified portfolio of stocks, bonds, or other securities. This diversification helps mitigate risk, as losses in one security may be offset by gains in another. Mutual funds are managed by professional fund managers who make investment decisions for the fund's shareholders. ETFs, on the other hand, are typically passively managed and track specific market indices. They trade on stock exchanges, offering flexibility and often lower fees than mutual funds. Understanding these instruments can empower you to decide where to place your money.

Compound interest is a powerful ally for investors. It is the process by which the earnings from your investments generate additional earnings over time. As your investment grows, the interest earned increases, leading to exponential growth. This principle underscores the importance of starting early. Even modest initial investments can grow significantly over the long term, thanks to the compounding effect. Recognize that time is on your side; leveraging it can yield substantial rewards as you build your portfolio.

Setting clear investment goals is crucial. Begin by distinguishing between short-term and long-term objectives. Short-term goals include saving for a vacation or a car, while long-term goals typically focus on retirement or a child's education. Understanding your risk tolerance is equally essential. Some individuals are comfortable with high-risk investments for the potential of greater returns, while others prefer stability, even if it means lower returns. Assess your willingness and ability to take risks, considering your income, savings, and financial responsibilities. This self-assessment will guide your investment choices and help you align them with your financial goals.

Choosing the correct investment accounts is a foundational step. Individual Retirement Accounts (IRAs) are essential for those without employer-sponsored retirement plans. Traditional IRAs offer tax deductions on contributions, while Roth IRAs provide tax-free growth on earnings. Both options have annual contribution limits, so understanding these nuances helps maximize your savings potential. Taxable brokerage accounts offer flexibility for investing in a wide range of securities without the tax advantages of IRAs. They allow you to start investing with smaller amounts and provide liquidity, as funds can be accessed anytime without penalties.

Starting with a small, diversified portfolio is a practical approach for beginners. Diversification spreads your investments across different asset classes, reducing risk and enhancing potential returns. Begin with a mix of stocks and bonds tailored to your risk tolerance and investment goals. Consider using robo-advisors, digital platforms that provide automated, algorithm-driven financial planning services. They offer personalized investment recommendations based on your financial situation and goals, often cheaper than traditional advisors. This guidance can be invaluable as you navigate the complexities of investing, providing confidence and clarity.

Interactive Element: Investment Goals Planner

Consider using an Investment Goals Planner to assist in setting clear investment goals. List your short-term and long-term objectives, risk tolerance, and desired time frames. This planner can help clarify your financial aspirations, keeping you focused and motivated as you build your portfolio. Regularly review and update your goals to reflect changes in your circumstances or priorities. Maintaining a visual record of your objectives reinforces the importance of disciplined investing and strategic planning.

As you embark on your investment journey, remember that the key is to start. Even small, consistent steps can lead to significant progress over time. You are well-equipped to achieve your financial goals with a clear understanding of investment fundamentals and a sound strategy.

2.2 Mid-Career Investment Opportunities

Your peak earning years present a golden opportunity to supercharge your investments. At this stage, you likely have more financial resources and more excellent stability, allowing you to maximize contributions to your retirement accounts. Take full advantage of employer-sponsored plans by contributing the maximum amount to your 401(k) or similar retirement accounts. Doing this not only boosts your retirement savings but also lowers your taxable income. Many employers offer contribution matching, which is free money added to your retirement fund. Ensure you contribute enough to capture the full match, as this is one of the most efficient ways to grow your savings. Beyond traditional retirement accounts, consider diversifying your portfolio with real estate investments. Real estate can provide both income through rentals and appreciation over time. It's a tangible asset that can hedge against inflation and diversify your investment portfolio. Explore options such as rental properties or real estate investment trusts (REITs), which allow you to invest in real estate without the hassle of managing properties directly.

Balancing risk and reward becomes crucial as you seek to maximize growth while protecting your assets. Rebalancing your portfolio is essential to align with your evolving goals and risk tolerance. Over time, the performance of different investments can shift your portfolio's balance, potentially exposing you to more risk than intended. Regularly review your asset allocation and adjust to maintain your desired balance between stocks, bonds, and other investments. As you move through your career, consider increasing your exposure to growth assets such as equities. These investments offer higher potential returns but come with increased volatility. Evaluate your risk tolerance and time horizon to determine the appropriate balance for your portfolio.

Employer-sponsored plans offer a range of benefits beyond just retirement savings. Many companies provide stock purchase plans, allowing you to buy company shares at a discounted rate, which can be an excellent opportunity to invest in your employer, especially if you believe in the company's long-term growth prospects. However, be cautious not to over-concentrate your investments in a single company, even if it's your employer. Diversification remains critical to managing risk. Review your employer's stock purchase plan details and consider how it fits into your investment strategy.

Exploring diversified asset classes can uncover new opportunities for growth and risk management. International stocks and bonds introduce geographic diversification, providing exposure to different economies and markets. Global investments can reduce reliance on the domestic market and enhance potential returns. Research international funds or ETFs that align with your investment objectives and risk appetite. Additionally, alternative investments such as commodities, private equity, or infrastructure funds can further diversify your portfolio. These assets often have a low correlation with traditional stocks and bonds, offering potential protection against market volatility. Assess the risks and benefits of each asset class and consider how they integrate with your overall strategy.

Visual Element: Portfolio Rebalancing Chart

To illustrate the importance of rebalancing, consider using a Portfolio Rebalancing Chart. This visual tool can depict how different asset classes have shifted over time and how rebalancing can bring them back in line with your strategic targets. By visualizing these shifts, you can better understand the impact of market movements on your portfolio and the necessity of periodic adjustments. Regularly updating this chart will help you maintain discipline and ensure your investments align with your financial goals.

2.3 Late Starters: Catch-Up Strategies

If you're entering the investment world later than you hoped, don't despair. There's still time to build a substantial portfolio, but it requires focused and accelerated strategies. One effective method is to make catch-up contributions to your retirement accounts. If you're 50 or older, take advantage of increased contribution limits for 401(k)s and IRAs. These additional contributions can significantly boost your retirement savings over a relatively short period. Consider allocating more of your income to these accounts, especially if you must meet your savings goals. This focused effort can help you close the gap and prepare adequately for your future. Simultaneously, explore high-yield savings strategies. These involve placing your money in accounts or instruments that offer competitive interest rates, allowing your savings to grow faster. Look for high-interest savings accounts, certificates of deposit (CDs), or money market accounts that offer better returns than traditional savings accounts. These options provide a safe place to park your cash while still earning a respectable rate of return.

Another approach is to focus on income-generating investments that provide steady cash flow, which can be particularly beneficial if you start late. Dividend-paying stocks are a prime example. They offer regular income through dividends, which can be reinvested to buy more shares, thus compounding your investment. Companies with a solid track record of paying and increasing dividends are financially stable, offering security alongside income. Additionally, consider bond laddering techniques. These techniques involve purchasing a series of bonds with varying maturities. As each bond matures, you reinvest the principal in a new bond at the end of the ladder. This strategy provides regular income from interest payments and helps manage interest rate risk by spreading the investment over different periods. It's a way to generate consistent income while maintaining capital preservation.

Tax efficiency is crucial when trying to accelerate your investment growth. Consider Roth IRA conversions as a strategy to enhance tax efficiency. By converting a traditional IRA into a Roth IRA, you pay taxes on the converted amount now, allowing your investments to grow tax-free and withdrawals tax-free in retirement. This conversion can be particularly advantageous if you expect to be in a higher tax bracket in the future. Tax-loss harvesting is another technique to consider. It involves selling investments that have lost value to offset gains in other areas of your portfolio. As a result, you reduce your taxable income and your tax bill, allowing you to reinvest the savings for additional growth. Implementing these tax-efficient strategies requires a thorough understanding of your financial situation and tax implications, so seeking professional guidance is often advisable.

Leveraging professional expertise can significantly optimize your late-stage investment strategies. Consider working with a financial advisor who specializes in retirement planning. They can provide personalized investment strategies tailored to your unique circumstances, helping you maximize your available resources. A skilled advisor will assess your financial situation, risk tolerance, and retirement goals to create a comprehensive plan that addresses your needs. They can also offer insights into complex financial instruments or strategies you need to become more familiar with, guiding you toward sound investment decisions. Personalized advice ensures that your investment strategy is aligned with your goals and risk profile, maximizing your chances of achieving a secure retirement.

2.4 Diversification and Asset Allocation Tactics

Diversification is a cornerstone of investment strategy, acting as a shield against the inherent risks of the market. By spreading your investments across various asset classes, you minimize the impact of poor performance in any area. This approach reduces volatility and enhances the potential for stable returns. Within asset classes, diversification involves holding a range of securities, such as a mix of different stocks or bonds, to avoid over-concentration in any sector or company. Consider geographic diversification as well. Investing in international markets mitigates country-specific risks and takes advantage of global growth opportunities. This buffers against domestic economic downturns and opens doors to emerging markets with high growth potential. Geographic diversification, therefore, serves as a dual-purpose strategy: risk management and growth enhancement.

You must consider your age and investment horizon for an effective asset allocation strategy. Younger investors typically allocate more to stocks, capitalizing on their long-term growth potential, while older investors might prioritize bonds for their stability and income. An age-appropriate asset allocation model adjusts the balance between growth and income as you progress through different life stages. Decide whether a dynamic or static allocation strategy suits your needs. A dynamic strategy involves regularly adjusting asset allocations based on market conditions or personal financial changes. At the same time, a static approach maintains a fixed allocation, relying on periodic rebalancing to manage risk. By aligning your asset allocation with your life stage and risk tolerance, you ensure that your investment strategy supports your financial goals and adapts to changing circumstances.

Rebalancing is a crucial practice for maintaining your desired risk level in a portfolio. Over time, market movements can cause your asset allocation to drift from its target, potentially exposing you to more risk than anticipated. Scheduled portfolio reviews, perhaps annually or semi-annually, allow you to assess and adjust your holdings back to their intended balance. Identify rebalancing triggers, such as a specific percentage deviation from your target allocation, that prompt you to make adjustments. Techniques for rebalancing can vary; some investors choose to sell overperforming assets and buy underperforming ones, while others use new contributions to restore balance. Rebalancing ensures that your portfolio remains aligned with your risk tolerance and investment objectives, guarding against unintended exposure to market volatility.

Index funds and ETFs offer a straightforward and cost-effective way to diversify your portfolio. These funds track broad market indices, providing exposure to various securities without needing active management. Their cost efficiency stems from lower management fees than actively managed funds, translating to higher net returns over time. Additionally, index funds and ETFs grant broad market exposure, capturing the market's overall performance rather than relying on the success of individual stocks. This approach simplifies the investment process and reduces the risk of significant losses from individual security failures. Index funds and ETFs attract investors seeking a low-maintenance, diversified portfolio, combining simplicity with robust market coverage.

2.5 Inflation-Proofing Your Portfolio

Inflation can erode the purchasing power of your hard-earned money over time, making it a critical factor to consider in your investment strategy. Historically, inflation has varied, with periods of high inflation reducing the value of cash holdings significantly. Understanding this trend is essential, as it impacts your actual returns—that is, the returns on your investments after accounting for inflation. While nominal returns might seem attractive on paper, their exact value diminishes if inflation outpaces them. For example, a 5% return on investment might sound promising, but if inflation is running at 3%, your real return is only 2%. So, one shouldn't underscore the importance of factoring inflation into your financial planning to ensure that your investment growth outpaces the rising cost of living.

To safeguard your portfolio against inflation, consider investment vehicles specifically designed for this purpose. Treasury Inflation-Protected Securities (TIPS) is a government-backed option that provides a fixed interest rate while their principal adjusts with inflation. This dual benefit ensures that your investment maintains its purchasing power over time. TIPS is a reliable choice for conservative investors seeking stability alongside inflation protection. Alternatively, commodities and precious metals, such as gold, offer another layer of defense. These assets often rise in value when inflation increases, acting as a hedge against currency devaluation. While commodities can be more volatile, their potential to preserve wealth during inflationary periods makes them valuable to a diversified portfolio.

Over the long term, investing in equities with solid growth potential can combat inflation effectively. Stocks have historically outpaced inflation, providing actual returns that enhance financial security. Companies that can raise prices and maintain profit margins during inflation are precious. These firms can pass on increased costs to consumers, preserving their earnings and, by extension, the value of your investment. Additionally, real estate serves as a robust hedge against inflation. Property values and rental incomes typically rise with inflation, offering income and asset appreciation. Real estate investments through direct ownership or REITs provide tangible assets to bolster your portfolio's resilience against inflationary pressures.

Regularly reviewing your portfolio is crucial to maintaining its inflation protection. Begin by periodically reviewing your inflation-sensitive assets, ensuring they align with your financial goals and market conditions. Adjust your asset allocation to maintain an optimal balance between growth and security as inflation expectations shift. Depending on the economic outlook, this might involve increasing your exposure to inflation-protected securities or high-growth equities. Staying proactive allows you to respond to changes in inflation trends and protect your portfolio from potential devaluation, preserving your wealth over the long term.

Textual Element: Inflation-Proofing Checklist

To assist in inflation-proofing your portfolio, consider using an Inflation-Proofing Checklist. This tool can help you evaluate your current asset allocation, identify inflation-sensitive investments, and track necessary adjustments. Systematically reviewing your portfolio with this checklist ensures that your investment strategy aligns with your financial goals and inflation expectations.

As you integrate these strategies into your investment plan, remember that protecting your assets from inflation is not a one-time task but an ongoing commitment. Regular adjustments ensure your portfolio remains robust against the eroding effects of inflation. By taking these steps, you safeguard your financial future, ensuring your investments continue to grow and provide the security you need for a prosperous retirement.

As you wrap up this chapter, you have explored various strategies to protect your investments from inflation's impact. From understanding inflation's effects to choosing suitable investment vehicles and making regular portfolio adjustments, these tools and insights prepare you to tackle inflation confidently. Transitioning into the next chapter, you'll delve into healthcare planning, a crucial aspect of securing your financial future.

Benjamin Graham – "The individual investor should act consistently as an investor and not as a speculator."

CHAPTER 3: NAVIGATING HEALTHCARE COSTS AND PLANNING

Imagine waking up to an unexpected medical bill that derails your carefully planned budget. It's a scenario many face, yet few anticipate. Healthcare costs have been relentlessly rising, fueled by various complex factors. Understanding these drivers is crucial in preparing for future expenses. Medical inflation rates continue to climb, often outpacing general economic inflation.

Consequently, services and treatments become more costly. Technological advancements, while improving care quality, usually come with a hefty price tag. Though beneficial, new diagnostic tools and therapies can increase the cost burden on patients. Meanwhile, policy changes can also impact what you pay for healthcare, whether aimed at expanding coverage or altering funding structures. Recognizing these factors helps you anticipate changes and prepare for their financial implications.

3.1 Navigating Future Healthcare Expenses

Forecasting your personal healthcare needs requires deep diving into your past medical expenses and family health history. This analysis provides a baseline for estimating future costs. Examine your medical records to identify patterns in your healthcare usage. Consider frequent consultations, recurring prescriptions, or chronic condition treatments. These insights offer a glimpse into your potential future needs.

Similarly, understanding your family health history can reveal potential genetic predispositions. If heart disease or diabetes runs in your family, factor these possibilities into your healthcare planning. By anticipating these needs, you can better estimate the resources required to maintain your health in retirement.

Accurate estimation of future healthcare expenses is made more accessible with the right tools and resources. Online healthcare cost calculators, such as the Health Insurance Marketplace Calculator by KFF, provide valuable estimates based on your income, age, and family size. These tools offer insights into potential premiums and subsidies, helping you budget effectively. Additionally, consulting with healthcare financial advisors can provide personalized guidance. These professionals can analyze your health history and financial situation to project future expenses. Their expertise can help you navigate the complexities of healthcare planning, ensuring you make informed decisions tailored to your circumstances.

Incorporating healthcare costs into your retirement plan is critical to financial security. Adjusting your savings goals to account for expected and unexpected medical expenses is one way you can achieve this objective. Allocate specific funds within your retirement savings dedicated to healthcare, such as by creating a separate account or fund earmarked for medical needs. Doing so ensures these costs are covered without compromising your broader retirement goals. Consider the impact of inflation on healthcare costs and adjust your savings targets accordingly. This proactive approach safeguards your financial future and provides peace of mind, knowing you are prepared for any health-related expenses that may arise in retirement.

Interactive Element: Healthcare Cost Planning Worksheet

To assist in this process, consider using a Healthcare Cost Planning Worksheet. This tool can guide you in estimating and organizing your future healthcare expenses. List potential costs, including premiums, copayments, and long-term care, alongside your estimated savings. Regularly update this worksheet to reflect changes in your health needs or financial situation. Maintaining a detailed record reinforces the importance of strategic planning and ensures you remain on track to meet your healthcare needs.

Understanding the multifaceted nature of healthcare costs empowers you to integrate these expenses into your overall retirement strategy. This chapter equips you with the knowledge and tools necessary to anticipate future healthcare needs and incorporate them into your financial planning. With careful preparation, you can face the future confidently, knowing you have taken the necessary steps to secure your health and economic well-being.

3.2 Maximizing Health Savings Accounts (HSAs)

Health Savings Accounts, or HSAs, offer a powerful tool in your retirement planning arsenal, particularly when managing future healthcare costs. HSAs stand out due to their triple tax advantage. First, contributions to the account are tax-deductible, reducing your taxable income. Second, the growth of your investment within the HSA is tax-free. Lastly, withdrawals for qualified medical expenses are also tax-free. This trifecta of tax benefits makes HSAs uniquely advantageous compared to other savings vehicles.

Moreover, HSAs provide flexibility in how you use the funds. You can cover various qualified medical expenses, from doctor visits and prescriptions to dental and vision care. This flexibility ensures you can address healthcare needs without dipping into other retirement savings. As you approach retirement, leveraging an HSA can significantly ease the financial burden of healthcare, giving you the confidence to face medical expenses head-on.

Contributing wisely to your HSA is crucial for maximizing its growth potential. The IRS limits how much you can contribute to your HSA each year. Annually maximizing these contributions is essential to exploit the account's full benefits. If you're 55 or older, you're eligible for catch-up contributions, allowing you to contribute an additional amount beyond the standard limit. This opportunity is particularly beneficial for those who started saving later in life, providing a valuable boost to your healthcare savings.

Once your HSA contributions are in place, consider investing the funds for long-term growth. Many HSAs offer investment options similar to retirement accounts, allowing you to invest in mutual funds, stocks, or bonds. By investing rather than leaving funds in a standard savings account, you harness the power of compound interest, potentially increasing your healthcare savings significantly by the time you retire. This strategy not only grows your funds but also provides a financial cushion to cover rising healthcare costs in the future.

During retirement, your HSA becomes an invaluable resource for managing medical expenses. One of the most practical uses is covering Medicare premiums and out-of-pocket costs. While you cannot use HSA funds to pay for Medigap premiums, they can be used for Medicare Parts B and D and Medicare Advantage premiums. This capability helps reduce the strain on your fixed retirement income, allowing you to preserve other savings for non-medical expenses. Additionally, HSAs allow for tax-free reimbursement of past medical expenses, provided you saved receipts. This feature gives you flexibility in managing your cash flow, as you can decide the best time to reimburse yourself, aligning with your overall financial strategy.

Use strategy while panning your HSA withdrawals, as it is critical to maximizing their tax benefits. Coordinate your withdrawals with other retirement income sources, such as Social Security or pension payments, to optimize your tax situation. By carefully timing your withdrawals, you can minimize your taxable income and potentially reduce your tax liabilities. Furthermore, avoid unnecessary HSA withdrawals. Taping into your HSA for non-qualified expenses is tempting, but doing so incurs taxes and penalties. Instead, use your HSA for healthcare-related costs, preserving its tax advantages. This discipline ensures that your HSA serves its intended purpose, providing a financial safety net for healthcare needs throughout retirement.

3.3 Long-Term Care Insurance: Is It Worth It?

Considering your retirement landscape, long-term care insurance might appear as a safety net worth exploring. The need for such insurance hinges on several risk factors. Age is a primary determinant—simply living longer increases the probability of requiring assistance with daily activities like bathing, dressing, or eating. Family history also plays a role; your chances might be higher if your relatives have needed long-term care. Existing health conditions, such as diabetes or heart disease, can accelerate the need for long-term care. When weighing your options, compare the costs of insurance against self-funding care. Without insurance, you might face out-of-pocket expenses that can deplete your savings rapidly. In some cases, the cost of long-term care can surpass even the most robust retirement savings, leading to financial strain.

Long-term care insurance offers specific features designed to mitigate these risks, yet understanding these features is crucial before deciding. Coverage types can vary significantly. Some policies cover care in a nursing home, while others extend to in-home care, assisted living, or adult day care. It's essential to know what each policy includes and excludes. Benefit triggers are another critical component, typically activated when you can no longer perform a specified number of daily activities independently. Familiarize yourself with these triggers, as they dictate when you'll start receiving benefits. Policy limits dictate the maximum amount payable over the policy's life, which can significantly impact your coverage. Inflation protection options are available in some policies, allowing your benefits to increase over time and keeping pace with the rising care costs. This feature can be invaluable, given the unpredictable nature of healthcare inflation.

Conducting a thorough cost-benefit analysis is essential in determining whether long-term care insurance aligns with your retirement plan. Start by evaluating premium costs against potential benefits. Premiums can vary widely based on age, health status, and the specific features of the policy. Consider your budget and whether you can sustain these payments long-term. Balance this with the potential benefits the policy offers. The policy could save substantial out-of-pocket expenses if you anticipate needing extensive long-term care. However, if the likelihood of needing care is low or you have other means to cover these costs, the premiums might outweigh the benefits. Assess the impact of this insurance on your overall retirement plan. It should provide peace of mind, knowing you have a safety net without compromising other financial goals. Consider how the policy fits into your broader strategy, ensuring it complements your existing financial framework rather than detracts from it.

Exploring alternatives to traditional long-term care insurance can provide additional perspectives. One option is hybrid life insurance and long-term care policies. These products combine the benefits of life insurance with long-term care coverage. If you don't use the long-term care benefit, your beneficiaries receive a death benefit. This dual-purpose coverage can offer more value, especially if you're hesitant about paying for insurance you might never use. Another approach is self-insurance, where you set aside a dedicated fund to cover potential long-term care costs. This strategy requires disciplined saving and investment, ensuring you have sufficient resources should the need arise. It provides flexibility, allowing you to allocate funds as needed, but requires careful planning to ensure adequate coverage. Each option has its merits and should be considered in the context of your financial situation and risk tolerance.

Navigating the world of long-term care insurance requires carefully examining your circumstances, risk factors, and financial goals. By understanding the nuances of coverage types, policy features, and alternative strategies, you can make informed decisions aligning with your retirement vision. Whether you choose traditional insurance, hybrid policies, or self-insurance strategy, the key is to ensure you're prepared for the potential costs of long-term care without jeopardizing your financial future.

3.4 Managing Chronic Health Conditions in Retirement

Managing chronic health conditions becomes vital to a fulfilling and active life as you plan for retirement. Creating a comprehensive healthcare management plan is your first step. Regular check-ups and preventive care form the backbone of this plan. Another crucial step is scheduling routine visits with your primary care physician and specialists to monitor and manage your conditions. These appointments allow for early detection of potential issues, making treatment more effective and less costly. Coordinating care among healthcare providers is another crucial aspect. Ensure that your doctors communicate with each other about your treatment plans and medications. This coordination helps prevent conflicting treatments and ensures a holistic approach to your health, ultimately enhancing your quality of life in retirement.

Budgeting for expenses related to chronic health conditions is essential to avoid financial strain. Prescription medication costs can increase quickly, especially if you require multiple prescriptions. Consider using generic medications where possible, as they are often significantly cheaper than brand-name drugs. Many pharmacies also offer discount programs or savings cards for recurring prescriptions. Your healthcare management plan should also account for medical equipment and specialist visits. Items like blood pressure monitors, mobility aids, or insulin pumps may be necessary, and their costs should be factored into your budget. Setting aside a portion of your retirement savings for these expenses can prevent them from eating into funds reserved for other areas of your life.

Leveraging available resources and support networks can provide valuable assistance in managing chronic conditions. Look for support groups tailored to your specific health issues. These groups offer a sense of community and shared experience, providing emotional support and practical advice. Accessing community healthcare services can also ease the burden of managing chronic conditions. Many communities offer free or low-cost physical therapy, nutrition counseling, or health education seminars. These services can supplement your healthcare management plan, providing additional support and resources. Staying informed about the resources available to you ensures you receive comprehensive care without overwhelming your finances.

Incorporating lifestyle changes is a proactive way to manage chronic conditions and improve overall health. Diet and exercise routines play a significant role. A balanced diet of fruits, vegetables, lean proteins, and whole grains can help manage symptoms and prevent complications. Consult with a nutritionist to tailor your diet plan to your health needs. Regular physical activity like walking, swimming, or yoga can improve mobility, strength, and cardiovascular health. Aim for 150 minutes of moderate-intensity weekly exercise, adjusted according to your ability and condition. Stress management techniques are equally important. Chronic stress can exacerbate health issues, so meditation, deep breathing, or tai chi can be beneficial. Integrating these routines into your daily life helps maintain control and well-being, allowing you to enjoy your retirement fully.

As you reflect on managing chronic health conditions, consider how these strategies fit into your retirement plan. This chapter has explored the importance of a healthcare management plan, budgeting for medical expenses, leveraging resources, and incorporating lifestyle changes. Together, these elements create a roadmap for maintaining your health and independence as you age. With careful planning and proactive management, you can face the future with confidence and vitality. In the next chapter, we will explore how to optimize your tax strategies to enhance your financial security in retirement. This knowledge will further empower you to make informed decisions that support a prosperous and fulfilling life.

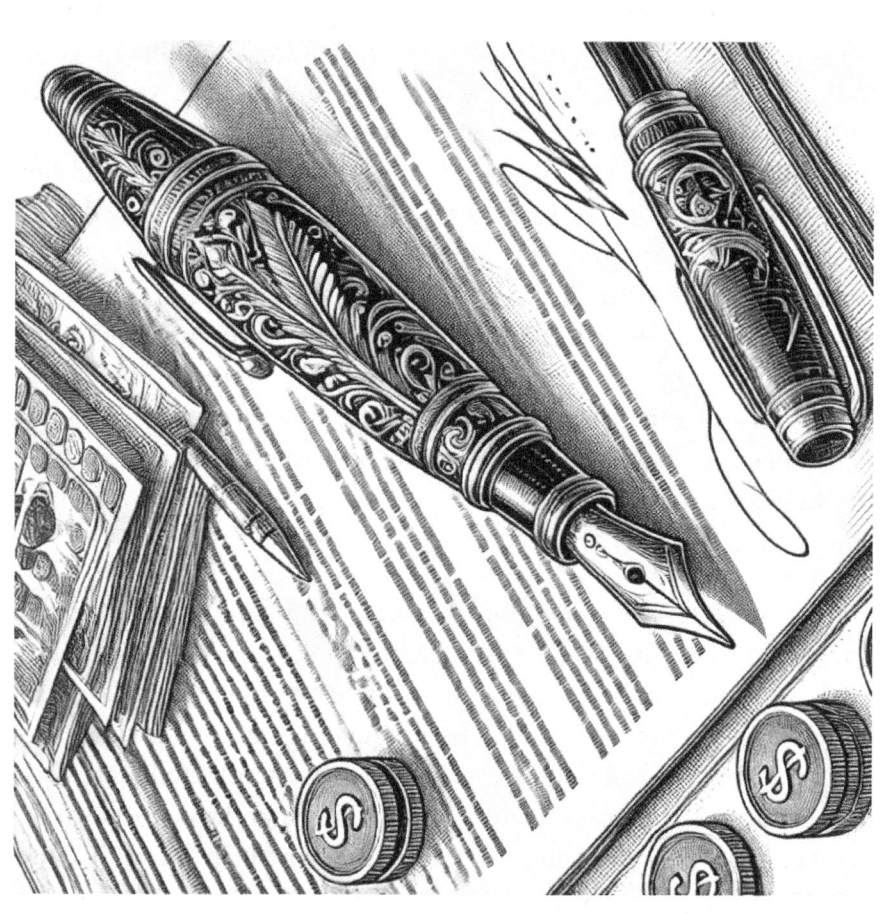

Indra Nooyi – "Whatever anybody says or does, assume positive intent. You will be amazed at how your whole approach to a person or problem becomes very different."

CHAPTER 4: OPTIMIZING TAX STRATEGIES FOR RETIREMENT

Taxes can feel like a maze that many struggle to navigate, especially when planning for retirement. Yet, mastering this aspect of financial planning can make a profound difference in your future. Consider the story of a mid-career professional who, by neglecting tax strategies, found his retirement nest egg significantly reduced by unexpected tax liabilities. This chapter will guide you in avoiding such pitfalls by understanding and leveraging tax-advantaged accounts, ensuring your hard-earned savings work efficiently.

4.1 Understanding Tax-Advantage Accounts

Tax-advantaged accounts are instrumental tools in building a robust financial future. These accounts, which include Traditional and Roth IRAs and 401(k) plans, provide substantial benefits by reducing your taxable income. Traditional IRAs allow you to make contributions with pre-tax dollars, meaning you get an immediate tax deduction, which can lower your current taxable income. This deferral of taxes continues until you withdraw the funds in retirement, at which point you pay taxes at your then-current rate. In contrast, Roth IRAs require contributions with after-tax dollars, but the significant advantage lies in the tax-free growth and withdrawals during retirement. You pay no taxes on the earnings or the withdrawals, provided you follow the rules set by the IRS. This distinction makes Roth IRAs particularly appealing for those who expect to be in a higher tax bracket in retirement.

401(k) plans, popular among employees, offer tax benefits. Contributions are made with pre-tax dollars, reducing your taxable income in the year of contribution. Like Traditional IRAs, taxes are deferred until withdrawal in retirement. Many employers match a portion of your contributions, effectively providing a return on your savings you cannot afford to miss. This employer match is a financial boon with tax implications as it grows tax-deferred alongside your contributions.

Maximizing your contributions to these accounts is essential for minimizing taxes and bolstering your retirement savings. As of 2023, the contribution limit for 401(k) plans has increased to $22,500, with an additional $7,500 catch-up contribution for those aged 50 and over (Source 1). For IRAs, the limit is $6,500, with a $1,000 catch-up provision. By reaching these limits, you substantially lower your taxable income while taking full advantage of tax-deferred growth. This strategy enhances your financial position both now and in the future.

During retirement, the tax benefits of these accounts continue to play a pivotal role. Roth IRAs shine due to their tax-free withdrawals, allowing you to access your savings without the burden of additional taxes. This feature is particularly advantageous when managing your retirement tax bracket. On the other hand, Traditional IRAs and 401(k) accounts require you to take Required Minimum Distributions (RMDs) starting at age 72. These distributions are taxed as ordinary income, which can impact your tax liability. Understanding this distinction is crucial for planning your withdrawals strategically to minimize taxes.

Choosing the correct account type hinges on your current financial situation and your expectations for retirement. Consider your current and anticipated tax brackets. If you expect to be in a higher bracket in retirement, a Roth IRA might be more beneficial, providing tax-free income when you need it most. Conversely, if you anticipate a lower tax rate in retirement, a Traditional IRA or 401(k) may be the better choice, as the immediate tax deduction can offer substantial savings now. Analyze your anticipated retirement income sources to determine which account aligns best with your financial strategy, considering factors such as Social Security benefits, pensions, and investment income.

Interactive Element: Tax-Advantaged Account Selection Quiz

Consider taking a Tax-Advantaged Account Selection Quiz to assist in this decision-making process. This interactive tool can guide you in evaluating your current financial situation, expected retirement income, and tax bracket considerations. By answering a series of targeted questions, you gain clarity on which account type may best suit your needs, ensuring your retirement savings strategy is tailored to your unique circumstances.

4.2 Roth Conversions: Timing and Benefits

Embarking on the path of Roth conversions can be a strategic move for optimizing your retirement savings. At its core, a Roth conversion involves transferring funds from a Traditional IRA to a Roth IRA. This conversion offers the potential for tax-free growth, a compelling advantage that can significantly impact your financial future. Once converted, these funds grow without the burden of taxes, allowing your investments to compound more effectively. Moreover, Roth IRAs do not require mandatory distributions during your lifetime, unlike Traditional IRAs. This flexibility means you can let your investments grow undisturbed or choose to withdraw strategically without being forced by age-related rules.

Timing your Roth conversion is central to maximizing tax efficiency. Ideally, such conversions should occur during years when your income is lower than usual. Conversion minimizes the immediate tax impact, as the converted amount is subject to income tax in the year of conversion. For example, if you experience a dip in your income due to a career change or a temporary break, it might be an opportune time to convert. Additionally, market downturns present another strategic window for conversion. When asset values are lower, the converted amount is less, reducing the associated tax burden. A lower tax burden means you pay taxes on a smaller amount, allowing for potential growth when the market rebounds.

Strategic planning is essential to minimize the tax implications of Roth conversions. Consider spreading conversions over multiple years instead of converting a large sum simultaneously. This approach helps avoid pushing yourself into a higher tax bracket, thereby managing your overall tax liability. Another tactic is to coordinate conversions with other income sources. By carefully selecting when to convert, you can prevent your total income from crossing into a higher bracket, a situation known as bracket creep. Start by understanding your income streams and doing careful financial planning to ensure conversions align with your broader tax strategy.

Despite the benefits, important considerations and potential pitfalls exist when planning Roth conversions. One significant factor is the impact on Medicare premiums. Converting large sums can increase your adjusted gross income, potentially raising your Medicare Part B and D premiums. This unexpected expense can offset some of the tax advantages of the conversion. It's essential to account for this in your planning to avoid surprises. State tax implications are another aspect to consider. Some states have different rules regarding the taxation of Roth conversions. Ensure you understand how your state handles these transactions to avoid unexpected liabilities. Consulting a tax professional can provide clarity and help tailor a conversion strategy to your specific circumstances.

4.3 Strategic Withdrawals from Retirement Accounts

Navigating the sequence of withdrawals from your retirement accounts can significantly impact your financial well-being. To optimize tax efficiency, consider withdrawing from taxable accounts first, then tax-deferred accounts like Traditional IRAs and 401(k)s, followed by tax-free accounts like Roth IRAs. This sequence allows you to take advantage of lower capital gains taxes and defer income taxes as long as possible. Balancing withdrawals is crucial to managing your overall tax liabilities. By carefully planning the order of withdrawals, you can minimize the risk of being pushed into a higher tax bracket, thereby preserving more of your wealth for the future. It's a strategic dance that requires foresight and precision, ensuring you meet your financial needs while keeping taxes in check.

Managing Required Minimum Distributions (RMDs) is another critical component in minimizing tax impacts. Once you reach the age of 72, the IRS mandates withdrawals from Traditional IRAs and 401(k)s, which are then taxed as ordinary income. Calculating accurate RMDs is essential to avoid hefty penalties—up to 50% of the amount not withdrawn. Ensure you understand the formula using your account balance and life expectancy factors. Many financial institutions provide RMD calculators or services to help with this. Once you take these distributions, consider reinvesting them. This strategy allows your money to grow, albeit in a taxable account. It's about maintaining the momentum of your financial growth while adhering to tax regulations.

Withdrawals can affect your tax brackets and overall tax liability. Each dollar withdrawn from a tax-deferred account adds to your taxable income, potentially pushing you into a higher bracket. Understanding where these thresholds lie is crucial. Plan your withdrawals around these thresholds to manage your tax bracket effectively. Combining withdrawals with tax credits and deductions can offset some tax impacts. For instance, if you have significant medical expenses or are eligible for certain tax credits, timing your withdrawals to maximize these benefits can reduce your taxable income. But before timing your withdrawals, one should carefully analyze their entire tax situation, ensuring that every strategic move is aligned with their financial goals.

Using withdrawals for charitable contributions offers an additional avenue to reduce taxes while supporting causes you care about. Qualified Charitable Distributions (QCDs) allow you to donate directly from your IRA to a charity, excluding the amount from your taxable income. This tactic fulfills RMD requirements and provides a tax-efficient way to support your philanthropic interests. Up to $100,000 can be donated annually without being included in your taxable income, making it a powerful tool for reducing tax liabilities. Exploring tax deduction strategies associated with charitable giving can further enhance your financial position. You can achieve personal and financial fulfillment by aligning charitable contributions with tax planning.

Textual Element: Tax-Efficient Withdrawal Checklist

Consider creating a Tax-Efficient Withdrawal Checklist to guide your strategy. This checklist can include steps for calculating RMDs, reviewing tax brackets, coordinating withdrawals with deductions, and planning charitable contributions. Regularly updating and reviewing this checklist ensures that your withdrawal strategy remains aligned with your evolving financial situation, helping you make informed decisions that optimize your tax outcomes.

Strategic withdrawals from retirement accounts require foresight and deliberate planning. By understanding the sequence of withdrawals, managing RMDs, and leveraging charitable contributions, you can design a withdrawal strategy that minimizes taxes and maximizes your financial security. This nuanced approach preserves your wealth and supports your broader retirement objectives, ensuring you enjoy the fruits of your labor with peace of mind.

4.4 Tax Implications of Social Security Benefits

Understanding how Social Security benefits are taxed is crucial for effective retirement planning. Taxing these benefits hinges on your provisional income, the sum of your adjusted gross income, nontaxable interest, and half of your Social Security benefits. This calculation determines whether your benefits will be taxed and to what extent. For individuals, if your provisional income falls between $25,000 and $34,000, up to 50% of your Social Security benefits may be taxable. If it exceeds $34,000, the taxable portion can rise to 85%. For joint filers, these thresholds are $32,000 and $44,000, respectively. Understanding your income relative to these thresholds helps you anticipate and plan for potential tax liabilities.

To minimize taxes on Social Security benefits, you can employ several strategies. One effective technique is income deferral, delaying specific income streams until you drop into a lower tax bracket. For example, you may postpone withdrawals from retirement accounts or delay other taxable income. By spreading your income more evenly over the years, you can keep your provisional income below the critical thresholds. Additionally, coordinating Social Security benefits with other retirement income sources can reduce tax exposure. For instance, if you anticipate a windfall from an investment or the sale of an asset, you may delay claiming Social Security benefits until the following year. This coordination requires careful planning but can significantly enhance your overall tax efficiency.

Other income sources can heavily influence the taxation of your Social Security benefits. Rental income, for example, adds to your provisional income, potentially pushing you into a higher tax bracket. If you own rental properties, it's vital to understand how this income interacts with your Social Security benefits. Similarly, investment income, mainly from taxable accounts, can substantially impact. Interest, dividends, and capital gains all contribute to your provisional income, affecting the overall tax on your benefits. Managing these income streams requires a strategic approach. Consider tax-efficient investment strategies, such as holding high-income-generating assets in tax-advantaged accounts or utilizing municipal bonds that offer tax-exempt interest.

Staying informed about potential policy changes affecting Social Security taxation is essential to your planning process. Legislative updates can alter tax thresholds, benefit calculations, or even taxation rules. For instance, changes in Social Security benefits tax treatment could arise from broader tax reform initiatives. Keeping abreast of these developments allows you to adjust your plans accordingly, ensuring that your financial strategy remains aligned with current laws. Monitoring government announcements, consulting with financial advisors, and participating in educational workshops are all effective ways to stay informed. Adjusting your plans in response to policy shifts safeguards your financial well-being and maximizes the benefits you receive.

Understanding the intricacies of Social Security taxation and strategically managing your income can significantly enhance your retirement experience. You can enjoy greater financial security by taking proactive steps to minimize taxes and staying aware of legislative changes.

4.5 Estate Planning and Tax Considerations

Taxes can heavily influence the effectiveness of your estate plan, making it crucial to account for them when transferring wealth. Estate taxes, often confused with inheritance taxes, are levied on the total value of a deceased person's estate before their assets are distributed to heirs. This tax can significantly reduce the wealth passed on, affecting your heirs' financial futures. Inheritance taxes, on the other hand, are paid by the inheritance recipients, and the rate can vary depending on the relationship to the deceased and the amount received. Gift taxes also play a role here; they are imposed on the transfer of property by one individual to another while receiving nothing or less than total value in return. Understanding these distinctions is vital, as each type of tax can impact your estate plan differently.

Consider strategies to minimize estate taxes to protect and preserve your wealth for future generations. One effective method is to utilize the lifetime gift tax exemption that allows you to give away a certain amount of money or assets during your lifetime without incurring gift taxes. By strategically gifting portions of your estate while living, you can reduce the taxable estate, thereby lessening the potential estate tax burden upon your passing.

Another powerful tool is setting up trusts to enhance tax efficiency. Trusts can be designed to manage and distribute your assets according to your wishes while providing tax benefits. For instance, a bypass trust, a credit shelter trust, can take advantage of the estate tax exemption to minimize taxes owed. Trusts offer flexibility and control, ensuring your assets are handled according to your desires while optimizing tax outcomes.

Estate planning should also incorporate the step-up in basis concept, a crucial consideration when passing on appreciated assets. This provision adjusts the value of an inherited asset to its market value at the time of the owner's death. As a result, capital gains taxes are minimized when the asset is sold because the gain is calculated from the stepped-up basis rather than the original purchase price. As a result, one can accumulate significant tax savings for your heirs. To maximize this benefit, consider holding onto appreciated assets until your passing, allowing your beneficiaries to take advantage of the step-up. This strategy can be particularly advantageous for real estate or stocks that have appreciated significantly over time.

Incorporating tax planning into wills and trusts can further enhance the efficiency of your estate plan. Charitable trusts, for example, fulfill philanthropic goals and offer substantial tax benefits. By establishing a charitable remainder trust, you can donate assets while retaining the right to income from them. This setup provides an immediate tax deduction and reduces the value of your taxable estate. Additionally, consider the generation-skipping transfer tax, which applies to transfers made to individuals more than one generation removed, such as grandchildren. Planning for this tax can involve setting up a generation-skipping trust to pass wealth while minimizing tax impacts. Properly structured, these tools ensure your estate plan aligns with your financial and familial objectives, optimizing legacy and tax outcomes.

Oprah Winfrey – "The more you praise and celebrate your life, the more there is in life to celebrate."

CHAPTER 5: DECIDING YOUR IDEAL RETIREMENT AGE

Picture this: you're standing at the edge of a new chapter, where the concept of time shifts from counting the hours at work to savoring moments filled with personal pursuits and leisure. The decision about when to retire is not just a question of age; it is a pivotal choice that shapes your future lifestyle and financial well-being. Many approach this decision with anticipation and apprehension, knowing it requires careful consideration of various factors. The notion of an "ideal" retirement age is unique to each individual and is influenced by financial readiness, personal goals, and lifestyle aspirations. This chapter delves into the crucial elements you must evaluate to identify your readiness for this significant transition.

5.1 Evaluating Financial Readiness for Retirement

Assess your current financial standing to determine if you are financially ready to retire by thoroughly reviewing your retirement savings accounts, including 401(k)s, IRAs, and any pensions you may have. Analyze these accounts to ensure they align with your retirement goals. Consider the balance, contribution rates, and projected growth over time. This evaluation offers a snapshot of your financial health and helps identify gaps that need addressing. As you review your savings, project your retirement income versus expected expenses. This projection is crucial, as it allows you to visualize how your savings will support your lifestyle. Consider fixed costs, such as housing, utilities, and healthcare, alongside discretionary expenses like travel and hobbies. This comprehensive view clarifies whether your current savings can sustain you throughout retirement.

Estimating your long-term financial needs is another essential step in the process. Consider the longevity risk, which refers to the possibility of outliving your savings. With advancements in healthcare and living conditions, people are living longer, which means your retirement savings must potentially last several decades. Life expectancy plays a critical role in this calculation, as it helps determine how long your savings should ideally last. Additionally, it factors in the impact of inflation on future expenses. Over time, inflation erodes the purchasing power of money, meaning you will need more funds to maintain the same standard of living. Strategies to mitigate this include investing in assets that outpace inflation and continuously reviewing your financial plan to account for changing economic conditions.

Identifying potential income sources is a crucial aspect of securing a stable retirement. Social Security benefits are a standard income stream for many retirees, with 77% relying on it as a source of income (Source 1). Understanding how these benefits integrate into your overall plan is crucial. Consider the timing of when to start receiving benefits, as this decision impacts the monthly amount you receive. Pension plans, if available, provide another layer of financial security. Evaluate the terms and conditions of any pensions to understand their benefits. Beyond these traditional sources, explore the possibility of annuities, which can provide a steady income stream throughout retirement. Additionally, rental income from properties can be a reliable supplement to your financial resources. Diversifying your income streams enhances financial resilience and reduces reliance on any single source, thereby fortifying your financial security.

Conducting a retirement income gap analysis ensures your income aligns with your expected expenses. This analysis helps pinpoint discrepancies between your projected income and the costs of maintaining your desired lifestyle. Early identification of these gaps allows you to implement strategies to close them, such as adjusting your savings or spending plans. If your analysis reveals a shortfall, consider increasing your savings rate or extending your working years to boost your retirement accounts. Alternatively, explore potential cost reductions, like downsizing your home or minimizing discretionary expenses. This proactive approach ensures that you confidently enter retirement, knowing your financial foundation is solid.

Interactive Element: Retirement Readiness Checklist

To assist in this comprehensive evaluation, consider utilizing a Retirement Readiness Checklist. This tool can guide you through each step, from assessing your financial standing to identifying income sources and conducting an income gap analysis. This structured checklist ensures that every aspect of your retirement planning is noticed. Regularly updating and reviewing this checklist can help you stay on track and make informed decisions as you approach retirement.

As you navigate these considerations, remember that the ideal retirement age is not a one-size-fits-all decision. It is a personalized journey shaped by your financial preparedness, lifestyle aspirations, and personal circumstances. By strategically assessing your readiness and planning, you pave the way for a fulfilling and secure retirement.

5.2 Balancing Personal Goals with Financial Realities

Retirement is often seen as the time to pursue personal dreams and aspirations finally, but aligning these goals with your financial capacity is crucial. Begin by examining what truly matters to you in retirement. You can start by distinguishing between lifestyle desires and economic constraints. Create a list of must-haves and nice-to-haves. Must-haves are non-negotiables—essentials such as healthcare, basic living expenses, and maintaining a certain standard of living. Nice-to-haves include luxury travel, a second home, or new hobbies. Prioritizing these elements helps you align your financial plan with your retirement goals. It's essential to be realistic about what your savings can support. If your financial analysis reveals a gap between your dreams and your budget, consider adjusting your goals to ensure they remain attainable. This approach keeps your retirement plans grounded and prevents financial stress.

Adapting to lifestyle changes is often necessary to align with financial realities. Downsizing your home or relocating to a more affordable area can significantly reduce living expenses, freeing up resources for other retirement activities. Many retirees find that a smaller house or a move to a less expensive locale lowers costs and simplifies their lifestyle. This change can also provide the opportunity to embrace a new community or climate, enhancing the quality of life. Additionally, consider reducing discretionary spending. Evaluate your current expenses and identify areas where you can cut back without sacrificing your quality of life. You may have to dine out less often, limit luxury purchases, or opt for more budget-friendly travel options. By consciously managing these expenses, you create more financial flexibility, allowing you to pursue your must-have goals with greater ease.

Health and wellness are fundamental considerations when planning the timing of your retirement. Anticipating healthcare needs and costs is vital, as they can significantly impact your retirement budget. Consider your current health status, ongoing medical conditions, and future healthcare needs. This foresight lets you plan for medical expenses, which often increase with age and factor in your physical ability for travel or hobbies. Many retirees look forward to traveling or taking up new activities, but these pursuits require a certain level of physical fitness. Assess your current health and anticipate how it might change over time. This evaluation helps you plan your budget and activities, ensuring they align with your physical capabilities. By prioritizing health, you enhance your ability to enjoy retirement fully.

Family and social dynamics play a significant role in shaping your retirement timing. Supporting dependents or grandchildren might influence your decision to retire earlier or later than planned. If you have financial responsibilities toward family members, consider how these obligations fit into your retirement plan. Extending your working years to ensure you can provide the necessary support. Alternatively, it might involve setting aside specific funds to fulfill these commitments. Maintaining social connections and community involvement is also vital for a fulfilling retirement. Consider how retirement will affect your social life and community engagement. Retirement often leads to changes in social networks, as work-related connections may diminish. Plan to maintain or expand your social circles through volunteer work, joining clubs, or attending community events. These interactions contribute to emotional well-being and help prevent isolation, a common challenge in retirement.

Balancing personal goals with financial realities requires thoughtful consideration and strategic planning. You create a realistic and attainable plan by aligning your retirement goals with your financial capacity. Adapting to lifestyle changes, prioritizing health and wellness, and incorporating family and social considerations ensure your retirement is financially secure and personally fulfilling. As you navigate these considerations, remember that flexibility and adaptability are key. Circumstances and priorities may change, and being prepared to adjust your plans is essential for a successful and satisfying retirement.

5.3 The Pros and Cons of Early Retirement

For many, the allure of early retirement is undeniable. The prospect of trading in a rigid work schedule for the freedom to explore personal interests is appealing. Imagine waking up without the pressure of deadlines and planning a day filled with activities you love. Early retirement offers the luxury of time—time to travel to destinations long on your bucket list, to dive into hobbies you have set aside, or to enjoy the peace of a day with no agenda simply. Moreover, stepping away from a demanding career can provide the mental space to embark on a second career or volunteer work, allowing you to pursue passions that align with your values. This shift can bring a newfound sense of purpose, whether mentoring young professionals in your field, contributing to community projects, or even starting a small business. Early retirement can catalyze reinvention, providing the flexibility to explore uncharted paths.

However, an early retirement comes with challenges that require careful consideration. One significant drawback is the reduction in Social Security benefits. If you claim benefits before reaching full retirement age, the monthly amount you receive will be permanently reduced, impacting your long-term financial security, especially as you age. Additionally, early retirement extends the time frame your savings need to last. With life expectancies increasing, you might have to stretch your resources over several decades, which can be daunting if your savings are not robust. The financial strain of covering healthcare costs is another concern, as retiring before eligibility for Medicare can mean higher insurance premiums. These economic challenges necessitate thoroughly examining your savings and income strategies to ensure sustainability.

Strategic planning is crucial to mitigate the financial risks associated with early retirement. Building a giant retirement nest egg before you leave the workforce can provide a buffer against unexpected expenses and market fluctuations, which might involve ramping up savings in the years leading to retirement, taking advantage of catch-up contributions, or maximizing investment returns through diversified portfolios. Exploring part-time work opportunities is another viable strategy. Not only can this supplement your income, but it also keeps you engaged and active, providing a sense of purpose and routine. Part-time work can be flexible, allowing you to balance leisure with earning, and can be tailored to your interests or skills, whether consulting in your former field or pursuing an entirely new venture.

Crafting a fulfilling lifestyle in early retirement requires thoughtful planning beyond just financial preparation. Engaging in lifelong learning or acquiring new skills can enrich your retirement experience. Whether you enroll in online courses, attend workshops, or participate in community classes, learning keeps your mind active and opens doors to new interests. This ongoing education can be intellectually stimulating and socially rewarding, as it often brings opportunities to connect with like-minded individuals. Pursuing passion projects or entrepreneurship can also provide a sense of achievement and fulfillment. Maybe you can finally write that novel, start a small business, or dedicate time to art or music. Such projects allow you to explore creativity and personal growth, ensuring your retirement years are productive and enjoyable.

Visual Element: Early Retirement Pros and Cons Chart

An early retirement pros and cons chart can be beneficial for visualizing the considerations of early retirement. This chart can outline the key benefits and challenges, providing a clear overview that aids decision-making. By weighing the pros and cons, you gain a balanced perspective on how early retirement aligns with your goals and financial realities. Regularly revisiting this chart can help refine your plans and ensure your retirement strategy evolves to meet changing circumstances.

Early retirement is a multifaceted choice that extends beyond the financial implications. It's about designing a life that reflects your aspirations while balancing the practicalities of long-term security. Each decision, whether it be your daily lunch order or early retirement, contributes to the tapestry of your after-retirement life, requiring both a visionary outlook and grounded pragmatism.

5.4 Strategies for Delayed Retirement Benefits

Extending your career beyond the traditional retirement age can bring substantial financial and personal advantages. One of the most notable benefits is the increase in Social Security payouts. For each year you delay claiming past your full retirement age, your benefits grow by a certain percentage until you reach 70. This increase can significantly bolster your monthly income, providing a more comfortable cushion as you retire. Additionally, if you continue working, you maintain access to employer-sponsored healthcare, often at a lower cost than available to retirees. This benefit can be invaluable in managing medical expenses, which tend to rise with age. By postponing retirement, you protect your financial health and ensure a more secure transition when you eventually retire.

Another compelling reason to delay retirement is the opportunity to enhance your retirement savings and benefits. Continued employment allows ongoing contributions to retirement accounts, such as a 401(k) or an IRA. These contributions increase your nest egg and benefit from tax-deferred growth, further expanding your financial resources. Moreover, many employers offer additional perks to retain experienced employees, such as increased matching contributions or bonuses. Leveraging these benefits can significantly impact your financial readiness for retirement. As you build your savings, consider reviewing your investment portfolio to ensure it aligns with your evolving risk tolerance and retirement timeline. This ongoing assessment helps maximize your returns and prepares you for the financial demands of retirement.

While the financial incentives for delaying retirement are clear, maintaining a healthy work-life balance during extended employment is crucial. As you age, the demands of a full-time job can become more taxing, making it essential to prioritize self-care and wellness. One way to achieve this balance is by negotiating flexible work arrangements with your employer. Many companies are open to accommodating seasoned professionals who wish to reduce their hours or work remotely. This flexibility allows you to manage your workload while still enjoying personal time and pursuing interests outside of work. Prioritizing self-care, such as regular exercise, healthy eating, and mindfulness practices, helps sustain your energy and enthusiasm, making your extended career both productive and fulfilling. By taking proactive steps to maintain balance, you ensure that your work remains a source of satisfaction rather than stress.

Despite the advantages, delaying retirement can also present challenges that need addressing. One potential downside is the risk of burnout and job dissatisfaction. As you extend your career, the routine and work pressures can lead to fatigue and diminished passion. To combat this, consider planning a gradual transition to full retirement. For instance, you can reduce responsibilities, delegate tasks, or mentor younger colleagues. Such changes can rejuvenate your interest and provide a sense of purpose, making your work environment more rewarding. Additionally, setting clear boundaries between work and personal life can prevent job-related stress from spilling over into your time. This balance is critical to maintaining enthusiasm and avoiding burnout as you approach retirement.

In addressing these challenges, keeping your long-term goals in perspective is essential. The decision to delay retirement should align with your broader vision for your post-career life. Regularly evaluate your financial and personal goals to ensure your extended career supports your objectives. By staying focused on the bigger picture and adapting as needed, you create a path that leads to a fulfilling and secure retirement. Balancing the benefits and challenges of delayed retirement requires thoughtful planning and an adaptable mindset, ensuring your later years are as rewarding as you envision.

In this chapter, we've explored the benefits and strategies for delaying retirement, emphasizing the importance of planning and maintaining balance. As you consider these factors, remember that the ideal retirement age is deeply personal, shaped by your unique circumstances and aspirations. You can confidently navigate this decision with careful consideration, ensuring a future that aligns with your goals and desires.

John D. Rockefeller – "Do not be afraid to give up the good to go for the great."

CHAPTER 6: CREATING A SUSTAINABLE RETIREMENT INCOME PLAN

Imagine the reassuring sound of a steady heartbeat—a rhythm you can rely on through life's uncertainties. Just as a consistent pulse signifies health and stability, a well-structured retirement income plan provides the financial security needed for peace of mind in your later years. Transitioning from a regular paycheck to relying on investments and savings can feel daunting. Still, with strategic planning, you can create an income stream supporting your desired lifestyle without fearing outliving your resources.

6.1 Building a Reliable Income Stream

Building a reliable income stream begins with diversification, a fundamental principle in managing financial security. Relying solely on one source, such as Social Security, can leave you vulnerable to policy changes or unexpected life events. Instead, blend multiple sources like Social Security, pensions, and personal savings to create a robust financial foundation. Each source offers distinct advantages and tax treatments, allowing you to optimize your income for stability and efficiency. Social Security provides a baseline of predictable income, bolstered by pensions, which add an extra layer of security with their steady payouts. Personal savings, grown over years of diligent contribution, offer flexibility and can be strategically withdrawn to supplement your income. Additionally, consider exploring part-time or freelance opportunities to enhance your financial portfolio. These roles provide additional income and keep you engaged and active, offering fulfillment beyond monetary gains.

Establishing a withdrawal strategy is critical in balancing income needs with longevity. The well-known 4% rule suggests withdrawing 4% of your retirement savings annually to ensure funds last throughout your retirement. However, this rule is just a starting point. Adjust your withdrawals based on spending habits and market conditions to avoid depleting your nest egg prematurely. For example, in years of strong market performance, you might withdraw a slightly higher percentage, while in lean years, you could scale back to preserve your principal. Regularly review your budget to ensure it aligns with your lifestyle and financial goals, making adjustments as necessary to maintain balance and sustainability.

Passive income opportunities provide an additional avenue for generating steady cash flow during retirement. Rental properties, for instance, offer consistent income through monthly rent checks while appreciating over time. This dual benefit makes real estate an attractive option for property management investors. Similarly, dividends from a well-diversified stock portfolio can supplement your income without drawing down your principal. Companies that consistently pay dividends often have stable earnings, providing reliable income streams. Diversification across sectors and industries can mitigate risks associated with economic downturns, ensuring your income remains resilient. By incorporating these passive income strategies, you create a multifaceted approach to retirement planning, enhancing both security and potential for growth.

Regularly monitoring and adjusting your income plans is essential to stay aligned with changing circumstances. Life is unpredictable, and your financial strategy should reflect that flexibility. Conduct annual income review meetings to assess your financial health, evaluating whether your current plan meets your needs and goals. These reviews provide opportunities to identify areas for improvement, such as reallocating assets or adjusting withdrawal rates. Adapting your strategy to unexpected expenses, such as medical emergencies or lifestyle changes, ensures you remain on track despite life's uncertainties. A proactive approach allows you to address challenges as they arise, maintaining control over your financial future.

Interactive Element: Income Diversification Checklist

Consider using an Income Diversification Checklist to guide your planning. This tool helps identify and organize your income sources, ensuring you maximize your potential. Regularly update this checklist to reflect changes in your circumstances, keeping your strategy current and effective.

Creating a sustainable retirement income plan requires thoughtful preparation and adaptability. You build a resilient framework that supports your desired lifestyle by diversifying income sources, establishing a strategic withdrawal plan, exploring passive income opportunities, and regularly reviewing your financial health. This comprehensive approach secures your financial future and empowers you to enjoy your retirement with confidence and peace of mind.

6.2 Understanding Annuities and Their Role

Annuities can be a cornerstone of your retirement strategy, offering a way to ensure a steady stream of income. Understanding the different types available is crucial to make the most of them. Fixed annuities provide a guaranteed payout, offering stability and predictability, much like a traditional pension. They're ideal if you seek certainty and want to know exactly how much you'll receive each month. Variable annuities, on the other hand, offer payments that fluctuate based on the performance of chosen investments, providing potential for growth alongside risk. They might suit your desire for higher returns if you're comfortable with market exposure. Immediate annuities start payouts almost instantly after a lump sum is invested. They can be an excellent choice if you're nearing retirement and want to convert savings into income quickly. Conversely, deferred annuities allow your investment to grow over time before payouts begin, which is suitable for those who have more time until retirement and want to maximize growth potential. Each type serves different financial goals, so aligning them with your strategy is critical.

The primary allure of annuities lies in their ability to deliver guaranteed lifetime income, acting as a financial buffer against the risk of outliving your savings. This assurance can transform your retirement experience, replacing uncertainty with confidence. By securing a fixed income, you can plan your expenses more effectively, knowing that some of your needs will always be met. Annuities also hedge against longevity risk, ensuring your funds don't dry as you age. This protection is precious in an era where people live longer, healthier lives. An annuity can act as a safety net, providing peace of mind that you won't outlive your financial resources and allowing you to enjoy your retirement without financial stress.

Despite their benefits, it's essential to be aware of the costs and fees associated with annuities, as these can impact your overall returns. Surrender charges are penalties for withdrawing funds early, which can be substantial, especially in the contract's early years. Understanding the terms of these charges is crucial before committing to an annuity. Administrative fees, which cover the cost of managing the annuity, also affect your returns. These fees vary widely, so comparing options is essential to ensure you get value for your investment.

Additionally, annuities often offer riders additional features that provide benefits like long-term care coverage or inflation protection. While these riders can enhance your annuity, they come with extra costs, so evaluating whether they're worth the added expense is essential. Balancing these costs with the potential benefits of the annuity is critical to making an informed decision.

Incorporating annuities into your retirement income plan requires careful thought and balance. Allocating some of your savings to annuities can provide a stable income floor, allowing you to cover essential expenses without worry. This strategy can complement other income sources, such as Social Security or pensions, creating a diversified income stream that enhances financial security. Balancing annuities with other investments is vital to maintain flexibility and adaptability. While annuities offer protection, they also tie up capital, so having liquid assets available for unexpected expenses or opportunities is crucial. By thoughtfully integrating annuities into your broader strategy, you can build a retirement plan that offers stability and growth, ensuring you're prepared for the future.

6.3 Pension Plans: Navigating Your Options

Pension plans can be a cornerstone of your retirement income, providing reliable funds. Understanding the different types of pension plans available is crucial for maximizing their benefits. There are primarily two categories of pensions: defined benefit and defined contribution plans. Defined benefit plans, often referred to as traditional pensions, promise a specified monthly benefit upon retirement. This amount is calculated based on factors like salary history and years of service. These plans offer predictable income, reducing the financial uncertainty often associated with retirement.

In contrast, defined contribution plans, such as 401(k)s, do not guarantee a specific benefit amount. Instead, the contributions are invested, and the final benefit depends on the plan's investment performance and the investment risk is shifted to the employee. Therefore, it is essential to manage these accounts actively. Additionally, cash balance plans combine features of both types, offering a defined benefit as a hypothetical account balance. These plans provide more portability than traditional pensions, often appealing to those who change jobs frequently. Understanding these distinctions helps you decide which plan best aligns with your retirement goals.

One cannot discount timing's influence on maximizing pension benefits. The age at which you start drawing from your pension can significantly impact your payouts. Most times, delaying the start date results in a higher monthly benefit as the funds accumulate over a more extended period. This strategy can be particularly advantageous if you plan to work past the standard retirement age. However, if you need funds earlier, starting sooner might be necessary. Weigh the pros and cons based on your financial needs and life expectancy. Survivor benefit options also require careful consideration. If you have a spouse or dependents, you might opt for a joint-and-survivor annuity, which continues to pay benefits to your beneficiary after your passing. While this typically reduces the monthly payout, it ensures continued support for your loved ones, providing peace of mind. Balancing these choices involves assessing your financial situation and future needs and ensuring that your pension supports a secure retirement.

Regarding pension plan payout options, several choices directly affect your retirement income. Opting for a lump sum payment gives you immediate access to your funds, allowing flexibility in managing your retirement finances. If you prefer to invest your funds or have significant short-term expenses, this option can appeal. However, disciplined financial management is required to ensure your funds last throughout retirement. Alternatively, annuity payments provide a steady income stream over time, reducing the risk of depleting your savings prematurely. This option suits those who value stability and predictability in their income. Single-life payouts offer higher monthly benefits but cease upon your death, making them suitable for individuals without dependents. While offering lower monthly benefits, joint-life payouts ensure that your spouse continues to receive income, safeguarding their financial future. Each option carries its trade-offs, so consider your circumstances and preferences when selecting the payout method that aligns with your retirement plan.

Integrating pensions with other income sources is a strategic way to enhance your financial security in retirement. Coordinating pension income with Social Security and savings withdrawals allows you to optimize your income streams, ensuring you have enough to cover expenses without drawing down your savings too quickly. For instance, you may delay Social Security benefits to increase your monthly payouts while relying on pension income initially. This approach can maximize your overall income over the long term. Adjusting other income sources based on pension reliability is also vital. If your pension is guaranteed and stable, you might take a more conservative approach to your investments, focusing on capital preservation. Conversely, if your pension has variable components or is subject to market fluctuations, you might diversify your investments more aggressively to offset potential income gaps. This balance ensures that your retirement income remains robust, adapting to changes in your financial landscape and personal needs.

6.4 Protecting Your Income from Market Volatility

Market volatility is like a sudden storm, unpredictable and sometimes severe, threatening the financial landscape you've carefully cultivated. Its impact can be particularly profound when you rely on your investments for a steady income during retirement. One of the most significant risks associated with market volatility is the sequence of returns risk, which occurs when the order and timing of investment returns negatively impact your portfolio's value, especially if withdrawals are made during market downturns. Even if the market eventually recovers, withdrawing funds when values are low can erode your capital, potentially leading to a shortfall in the later years of retirement. Economic downturns compound this issue, as they often force you to withdraw more from your savings to cover expenses, thereby depleting your assets faster than anticipated.

Implementing robust risk management strategies is crucial to shield your retirement income from such volatility. Maintaining a well-diversified portfolio is your first line of defense. By spreading investments across various asset classes, you reduce the impact of any single asset's poor performance on your overall portfolio. Diversification not only helps stabilize returns but also positions you to benefit when different sectors of the market perform well. Beyond diversification, consider incorporating a cash reserve specifically for market downturns. This reserve acts as a buffer, allowing you to draw from cash rather than selling investments at a loss during turbulent times. It provides flexibility and ensures that your long-term investments have the opportunity to recover, preserving your capital for future growth.

Adopting safe withdrawal strategies is another critical component in protecting your retirement assets. One approach is to use dynamic withdrawal strategies, which adjust the amount you withdraw based on current market conditions and your portfolio's performance. By being flexible and reducing withdrawals during down markets, you help preserve your principal and enhance the longevity of your savings. The guardrails approach is a dynamic strategy that sets predefined limits or "guardrails" on withdrawals. If your portfolio value falls below a certain threshold, you reduce your withdrawals to prevent further erosion. Conversely, you may allow larger withdrawals if your portfolio grows beyond expectations. This method provides a structured yet adaptable framework that aligns with market realities and personal financial needs.

Regular portfolio reviews and adjustments are essential to ensure your investment strategy remains aligned with market conditions and financial goals. Regularly rebalancing your assets helps maintain your desired asset allocation, preventing undue exposure to riskier investments. For instance, if a particular asset class outperforms others, your portfolio might become too heavily weighted in that class, increasing risk. Rebalancing involves selling some overperforming assets and buying underperforming ones to restore balance. This disciplined approach keeps your investments aligned with your risk tolerance and objectives. Engaging in portfolio stress testing further enhances your preparation. This process involves simulating various market scenarios to evaluate how your portfolio might perform under different conditions. By understanding potential vulnerabilities, you can make informed adjustments, ensuring your strategy is resilient against future volatility.

Market volatility, while inevitable, doesn't have to derail your retirement plans. By understanding the risks and implementing strategies to manage and mitigate them, you can protect your income and maintain financial stability. This chapter has explored the importance of diversification, the utility of cash reserves, the flexibility of dynamic withdrawal strategies, and the necessity of regular portfolio reviews. Together, these elements form a comprehensive approach to safeguarding your retirement income against the unpredictable nature of the markets. As you continue to navigate your retirement journey, these strategies will empower you to face financial uncertainties with confidence and resilience.

In the next chapter, we will explore estate planning and legacy building, ensuring that your financial legacy is preserved and passed on to future generations.

Make a Difference with Your Review

Unlock the Power of Generosity

"The best way to find yourself is to lose yourself in the service of others." – Mahatma Gandhi

When we help others, we create ripples of kindness that can change lives. Your experience with *The Retirement Planning Accelerator* could be the encouragement someone else needs to take control of their future.

Would you help someone just like you—someone who dreams of a comfortable retirement but doesn't know how to get started?

My mission with this book is to make retirement planning simple, clear, and approachable for everyone. But to reach even more people, I need your help.

Most people decide on books based on reviews. Your words could inspire another person to begin their journey toward a secure and joyful retirement.

Leaving a review costs nothing, takes less than a minute, and could make a huge difference. Your review could help:

- ...one more family feel confident about their future.
- ...one more hard worker prepare for the retirement they deserve.
- ...one more reader feel empowered to take charge of their finances.
- ...one more person transform their dreams into plans.

To make a difference, simply scan the QR code below or click here to leave your review:
[https://www.amazon.com/review/review-your-purchases/?asin=BOOKASIN]

If you love helping others, you're my kind of person. Your review could guide someone toward the peace of mind they've been searching for.

Thank you from the bottom of my heart for being part of this journey. Together, we're helping others achieve the retirement they've worked so hard for.

Warmly,
Jon J. McKenzie
Author of *The Retirement Planning Accelerator*

Steve Jobs – "The people who are crazy enough to think they can change the world are the ones who do."

CHAPTER 7: ESTATE PLANNING AND LEGACY BUILDING

Consider a family torn apart by the absence of a clear estate plan. The patriarch, a successful entrepreneur, passed away unexpectedly, leaving behind a legacy of wealth but no instructions on how it should be distributed. The lack of a will led to disputes among his children, with each believing they understood his wishes. Although unfortunate, this tale is all too common and highlights the critical role of estate planning in preserving wealth and family harmony. Estate planning is not just about dividing assets; it is about ensuring that your wishes are honored, your loved ones are cared for, and your legacy endures. At its heart, estate planning is a proactive approach to managing what happens to your assets after you are gone, and it starts with understanding the fundamental tools available: wills and trusts.

7.1 The Basics of Wills and Trusts

A will is a legal document that outlines how your assets should be distributed after your death. It is your opportunity to ensure that your possessions, from sentimental heirlooms to significant investments, reach the people or organizations you care about most. More than just a list of beneficiaries, a will can include instructions for guardianship of minor children, providing peace of mind that they will be cared for by someone you trust. This aspect of a will is crucial for parents, as it allows them to choose who will raise their children if they can no longer do so. A well-crafted will can clarify your intentions, minimize potential conflicts among your heirs, and provide a clear roadmap for executing your final wishes.

On the other hand, trusts offer different kinds of control and flexibility in estate planning. Unlike a will, which only takes effect after death, a trust can manage and distribute your assets during your lifetime. Trusts come in various forms, each serving distinct purposes. A revocable trust, also known as a living trust, can be altered or revoked by the creator during their lifetime, offering flexibility and control. It allows you to manage your assets while alive and designate how they should be handled after death without the need for probate—a legal process that can be lengthy and public.

In contrast, an irrevocable trust, once established, cannot be changed without the beneficiary's consent, protecting from creditors and potential tax advantages. Special needs trusts are designed to support beneficiaries with disabilities without affecting their eligibility for government benefits, ensuring they receive the necessary care and resources. Living trusts benefit complex estates, allow for the seamless transfer of assets, and reduce administrative burdens on your heirs.

Drafting a comprehensive will is a critical step in estate planning, and it requires careful consideration of several vital elements. Start by naming an executor, a trusted individual responsible for overseeing the distribution of your assets according to your will. This person should be organized, reliable, and capable of managing responsibilities. Next, specify how your assets should be distributed. Clearly outline who receives what: family members, friends, or charitable organizations. Be specific to avoid misunderstandings and ensure your wishes are carried out accurately. In today's digital age, including digital assets in your will is essential. Ensure that you include online accounts, digital currencies, social media profiles, and any other virtual property you own in your will. Naming a digital executor can help manage these assets, ensuring they are distributed according to your wishes and protecting your digital legacy.

Once your will and any associated trusts are established, the work doesn't stop. Keeping these documents current is essential to ensure they remain effective and reflect your wishes and circumstances. Life is constantly changing—marriages, divorces, births, deaths, or significant financial changes can all affect your estate plan. Regularly review and update your estate planning documents, ideally every three to five years or after any major life event, to ensure they align with your current situation and intentions. This proactive approach prevents outdated instructions from creating confusion or conflict among your beneficiaries. Additionally, stay informed about changes in laws that might impact your estate plan. Legal requirements can evolve, and adjustments to your documents may be necessary to maintain their validity and effectiveness.

Textual Element: Estate Planning Checklist

To assist in organizing and maintaining your estate plan, consider using an Estate Planning Checklist. This tool can guide you through drafting a will, establishing trusts, and regularly reviewing your documents. It can remind you of the critical steps and considerations, helping you ensure that all aspects of your estate plan are addressed and updated as needed. Following this checklist, you can take a structured approach to estate planning, providing clarity and peace of mind for you and your loved ones.

Estate planning is more than just financial security; it's about ensuring that your legacy is protected and your wishes are respected. By understanding the roles of wills and trusts, drafting comprehensive legal documents, and keeping them up to date, you can create a plan that preserves your legacy and provides for your loved ones. Engage with the process proactively, and you can confidently navigate the complexities of estate planning.

7.2 Avoiding Common Estate Planning Pitfalls

Despite its importance, estate planning is often riddled with pitfalls that can derail your intentions and create unnecessary burdens for your loved ones. One of the most prevalent mistakes is failing to plan for incapacity. Many people focus solely on what happens after death, neglecting the crucial period when you might be alive but unable to make decisions for yourself. Without a plan, such as a power of attorney or a healthcare proxy, your family might face legal hurdles to make critical decisions about your healthcare and finances. This oversight can lead to stress and confusion, potentially leaving your wishes fulfilled.

Additionally, overlooking beneficiary designations is another common error. These designations on accounts like retirement funds or life insurance policies often supersede the instructions in your will. Failing to update them after major life events—such as a marriage, divorce, or childbirth—might lead to unintended beneficiaries receiving your assets, contradicting your current wishes.

Family disputes are another significant risk in estate planning, often arising from unclear intentions or perceived inequalities. Ensure that you communicate your intentions clearly and transparently to avoid future familial conflicts. Discuss your plans openly with your family, explaining your decisions and their reasoning. This dialogue can prevent misunderstandings and reduce the potential for resentment. Regarding asset distribution, consider the difference between equal and equitable distribution. Equal distribution means dividing assets uniformly, which might seem fair but could overlook individual circumstances. Equitable distribution, on the other hand, considers each heir's specific needs and situations, aiming for fairness rather than equality. For example, one child might have more significant financial needs due to a lower-paying job or health issues, while another might already be financially secure. Addressing these nuances can help tailor your estate plan to reflect your values and your family's realities.

Liquidity is another critical aspect often neglected in estate planning. Sufficient liquidity in your estate is essential for covering expenses such as taxes, debts, and immediate costs following your passing. Your heirs can settle these obligations with adequate liquid assets, potentially leading to the forced sale of valuable but illiquid assets like real estate or business interests. Planning for taxes and debts is an integral part of ensuring liquidity. Consider the potential tax liabilities and outstanding debts your estate might incur. Setting aside specific funds or purchasing life insurance can provide the necessary liquidity to cover these costs. Balancing liquid and illiquid assets in your estate is vital. Liquid assets, such as cash, stocks, or bonds, can be quickly converted to cash without significant loss of value. In contrast, while potentially valuable, illiquid assets might take time to sell and could fluctuate in market value. Ensuring a healthy mix of both can ease the financial burden on your heirs.

Understanding the tax implications of your estate planning decisions is crucial in preserving the value of your estate for your beneficiaries. Estate tax thresholds and exemptions can significantly impact what your heirs receive. Federal estate taxes apply to estates exceeding a specific value, and the exemption amount can vary based on current laws. It's essential to stay informed about these thresholds and plan accordingly. One strategy to reduce estate size and potential tax liabilities is gifting during your lifetime. Gifting assets to heirs can lower the value of your estate, potentially keeping it under the taxable threshold.

Additionally, gifting allows your beneficiaries to benefit from your generosity during your lifetime. However, it is essential to know the annual gift tax exclusion limits and how they apply to your gifting strategy. Careful planning and consultation with a tax professional can help you navigate these complexities, ensuring your estate plan is as tax-efficient as possible.

Estate planning requires careful attention to avoid common pitfalls and ensure your intentions are realized. By addressing potential incapacity, maintaining clear communication, providing liquidity, and understanding tax implications, you can create a plan that upholds your wishes and safeguards your legacy for future generations.

7.3 Building a Legacy: More Than Just Money

When you think about the legacy you'll leave behind, it's about more than just financial wealth. It's about the values and beliefs that define you and what you stand for. Consider what you want your legacy to represent. Is it honesty, kindness, or resilience? It could be the value of hard work or the belief in lifelong learning. By identifying these core principles, you can ensure they continue influencing your family long after you're gone. Education and mentorship are powerful tools in this process. Share your knowledge and life lessons with younger generations, guiding them through their paths. Whether it's teaching a skill, offering career advice, or simply imparting wisdom gained through experience, these acts of mentorship can leave a lasting impact.

Family values and traditions play a crucial role in shaping your legacy. They are the threads that weave together the fabric of family identity, providing continuity and connection across generations. Establishing a family mission statement can help clarify these values. This statement is a guiding principle, outlining what your family stands for and aspires to achieve. It's a collective vision that everyone can rally around, reinforcing a sense of unity and purpose. In addition to a mission statement, maintaining family traditions is vital. These customs—a holiday celebration, a weekly dinner, or an annual trip—create shared memories and foster a sense of belonging. Through storytelling, you can pass down these traditions and the stories behind them, ensuring they remain vibrant and meaningful.

Creating a family governance structure can further solidify your legacy. This framework provides a formalized approach to family decision-making, ensuring everyone's voice is heard and considered. Regular family meetings or councils can facilitate open communication and collaborative problem-solving. These gatherings offer a space to discuss important issues, celebrate successes, and plan for the future. Establishing clear roles and responsibilities within the family creates a more organized and harmonious environment. Family charters can also play a significant role. These documents outline the family's core values, rules, and procedures as a reference point for future generations. They provide clarity and consistency, helping to navigate potential conflicts and maintain family cohesion.

Storytelling is a powerful tool in preserving family history and legacy. Through stories, you can bring to life the experiences, challenges, and triumphs that have shaped your family. Documenting these stories ensures they are preserved over time. Consider writing them down in a family journal or creating a digital archive. These records can serve as a rich resource for future generations, offering insights into their heritage and identity. Legacy letters or videos can also be a meaningful way to communicate your thoughts and feelings to your loved ones. These personal messages allow you to express gratitude, share lessons learned, and offer guidance for the future. They become cherished keepsakes, providing comfort and inspiration for years to come.

Building a legacy that transcends financial wealth involves intentional and thoughtful actions. It's about instilling values, fostering traditions, and creating structures that support family unity and growth. By focusing on these elements, you can ensure that your legacy is one of lasting significance, touching the lives of those you leave behind.

7.4 Philanthropy and Charitable Giving in Retirement

Retirement opens a window for personal reflection and a chance to focus on giving back to the community. Engaging in philanthropy can be a gratifying aspect of life beyond work, offering numerous ways to contribute to causes that resonate with your values. Donor-advised funds (DAFs) are an excellent option, allowing you to contribute assets to a fund, receive an immediate tax deduction, and then distribute the funds to charities of your choice over time. This flexibility lets you strategically plan your giving, ensuring that your contributions have the most significant impact. Charitable remainder trusts offer another avenue, providing you with income during your retirement while eventually benefiting your chosen charity. This dual benefit can be particularly appealing as it balances financial security with altruism. Beyond monetary contributions, volunteerism and community involvement are powerful ways to give back. Volunteering your time and skills enriches the community and adds a new dimension of fulfillment to your retirement.

The benefits of charitable giving extend beyond the financial realm, touching on personal fulfillment and community impact. Many retirees find that giving brings a sense of purpose and satisfaction, knowing they are making a difference in the lives of others. Tangible financial benefits, such as tax deductions for charitable contributions, often accompany this fulfillment. These deductions can reduce your taxable income, providing an economic incentive alongside the intrinsic rewards of giving. Moreover, your involvement in charitable activities can create a ripple effect in the community, inspiring others to contribute and fostering a culture of generosity and support. By aligning your giving with your values, you reinforce the impact of your contributions, ensuring they resonate personally and within the broader community.

Developing a charitable giving plan is essential to ensure your philanthropic efforts are focused and effective. Start by setting clear priorities and identifying the causes that matter most to you. Whether it's education, healthcare, the environment, or another passion, having a defined focus helps direct your resources where they can do the most good. Budgeting for charitable donations is another crucial step. Determining how much you can afford to give while maintaining your financial security and setting aside a specific percentage of your retirement income or allocating some of your investment returns to charity can be the first step. A structured plan ensures that your giving is consistent and sustainable, allowing you to support your chosen causes over the long term. By approaching philanthropy with the same strategic mindset you apply to other aspects of financial planning, you maximize the potential impact of your contributions.

Involving family in your philanthropic endeavors can add another layer of meaning and engagement. Establishing a family foundation provides a formal structure for collaborative giving, allowing family members to decide which causes to support and how to allocate resources. This involvement can strengthen family bonds and instill a sense of shared purpose. Collaborative decision-making in charitable activities encourages open dialogue and fosters cooperation and understanding among family members. It also presents an opportunity to pass down values and inspire future generations to continue the legacy of giving. By involving your family in philanthropy, you create a tradition of generosity and social responsibility, ensuring that your passion for helping others lives on through your descendants.

Philanthropy in retirement is about more than financial contributions; it is a path to personal growth, community connection, and lasting impact. You can create a meaningful and enduring legacy by exploring various philanthropic opportunities, understanding the benefits of giving, developing a structured plan, and involving your family. This approach enhances your retirement experience and contributes to a better world, aligning your values with tangible actions that make a difference. As you transition to the next chapter, consider how these philanthropic principles can complement your retirement strategy, enriching your life and those you touch.

Warren Buffett – "Price is what you pay. Value is what you get."

CHAPTER 8: REAL ESTATE INVESTING FOR RETIREMENT

Consider the story of Susan and Mark, a couple who started investing in rental properties in their late 30s. Over two decades, they acquired four rental properties that now generate enough income to cover most of their living expenses in retirement. By leveraging the power of real estate, Susan and Mark created a sustainable income stream that has given them financial independence and the freedom to enjoy their retirement on their terms.

8.1 Introduction: The Power of Real Estate

Regarding retirement planning, investing in real estate can be one of the most impactful strategies for building long-term wealth. Unlike the volatility often seen in the stock market, real estate offers stability and consistent growth, making it an attractive option for those seeking financial security in retirement. But real estate investing is more than buying a property and hoping its value increases—it's about leveraging assets to generate income, manage risk, and create a safety net for your future.

This chapter will explore using real estate to boost your retirement savings. We will discuss different types of real estate investments, how to generate passive income, the benefits and risks involved, and practical strategies for building a real estate portfolio that aligns with your retirement goals. We'll also share real-life examples and expert insights to help you confidently navigate the world of real estate investing.

Real estate investing offers several unique benefits that make it an effective tool for retirement planning. These include generating passive income, the potential for property appreciation, and significant tax advantages. Real estate also provides diversification, helping you mitigate the risks of putting all your savings into stocks or other investments.

8.2 Types of Real Estate Investments

There are several different types of real estate investments that you can use to build wealth for retirement. Each type has its unique characteristics, benefits, and risks. Let's take a closer look at some of the most common options.

Residential rental properties are one of the most common types of real estate investments, including single-family homes, duplexes, and multi-family units. The primary goal of investing in residential rentals is to generate consistent rental income while also benefiting from property appreciation over time.

Another type is commercial rental properties. Commercial properties include office buildings, retail spaces, and warehouses. While the initial investment in commercial properties may be higher than residential properties, the potential returns are often greater. Commercial leases tend to be longer, providing more stable income, but they can also require more involvement and property management expertise.

Short-term vacation rentals, such as those listed on Airbnb or VRBO, can provide significant income if the property is in a desirable location. However, they also require more active management, and the income may be seasonal, which provides a different consistent income from long-term rentals.

If you want exposure to real estate without the hassle of managing properties, REITs are a great option. REITs are companies that own, operate or finance income-producing real estate. By purchasing shares of a REIT, you can earn a portion of the income generated by the underlying properties, including residential, commercial, or industrial properties. REITs are traded on major stock exchanges, making them a convenient way to invest in real estate while maintaining liquidity. Real estate crowdfunding allows individual investors to pool their money for larger projects like apartment complexes or commercial developments. Crowdfunding platforms enable investors to participate in deals they might not otherwise be able to afford independently. While real estate crowdfunding can offer attractive returns, it's essential to understand that these investments may be less liquid and come with more risk than traditional rental properties or REITs.

Last but not least, house flipping involves buying properties that need renovations, making improvements, and then selling them for a profit. While house flipping can be profitable, it requires significant time, effort, and expertise. Understanding renovation costs, the local real estate market, and potential resale values is essential before embarking on a house-flipping project.

8.3 Generating Passive Income Through Rental Properties

One of the most significant advantages of real estate investing is generating passive income. Rental properties, in particular, can provide a steady stream of income that can help cover living expenses in retirement.

Consider Jim, who purchased his first rental property at age 40. Over the next 15 years, he acquired three more properties. By the time Jim was ready to retire, the rental income from his properties was enough to cover his mortgage, utilities, and other expenses, allowing him to enjoy his retirement without worrying about money. The key to Jim's success was a combination of careful planning, buying properties in desirable neighborhoods, and effectively managing his rental units.

To generate passive income from rental properties, it's essential to:

Choose the Right Location. Location is one of the most critical factors in real estate investing. Look for properties with solid job growth, good schools, and low crime rates. These factors will help ensure that your property remains in demand, making finding tenants easier and keeping vacancy rates low.

Screen Tenants Carefully. Finding reliable tenants is essential for maintaining consistent rental income. Conduct thorough background checks, verify employment and income, and contact previous landlords to ensure prospective tenants are responsible and capable of paying rent on time.

Maintain Your Property. Keeping your property in good condition helps attract quality tenants but also helps preserve the property's value over time—budget for regular maintenance and repairs to avoid costly issues down the road.

Leverage Property Management Services. If managing rental properties sounds too much work, consider hiring a property management company. While this will reduce your net rental income, it can also save you time and reduce stress, especially if you own multiple properties.

8.4 The Benefits of Real Estate Appreciation

Another critical benefit of real estate investing is appreciation. Over time, the value of real estate tends to increase, providing an opportunity to build wealth through capital gains. While economic conditions and local market trends can influence real estate appreciation, historical data shows that property values generally rise over the long term.

For example, Sarah purchased a single-family home for $200,000 in a growing neighborhood. Fifteen years later, the property's value had appreciated to $400,000. In addition to the rental income she earned over the years, Sarah benefited from the significant increase in the property's value, contributing to her overall net worth.

It's important to note that real estate appreciation is not guaranteed, and property values can fluctuate based on market conditions. However, investing in areas with solid fundamentals—such as job growth, population growth, and infrastructure development—increases your chances of benefiting from appreciation.

8.5 Tax Advantages of Real Estate Investing

Real estate investing has several tax advantages that can help you maximize your retirement savings. These include:

Depreciation: The IRS allows you to depreciate the value of your rental property over time, which can reduce your taxable income. Depreciation is a non-cash deduction, meaning you can reduce your tax liability without spending money.

Deductions: Real estate investors can deduct many expenses for owning and managing rental properties, including mortgage interest, property taxes, insurance, maintenance, and property management fees. These deductions can significantly reduce your taxable income, allowing you to keep more of your rental income.

1031 Exchange: A **1031 exchange** allows you to defer paying capital gains taxes when you sell an investment property as long as you reinvest the proceeds in a similar property within a specific timeframe. This loophole can be a powerful tool for building wealth, as it allows you to leverage the appreciation of your properties without paying taxes on the gains until you eventually sell without reinvesting.

8.6 Real Estate as a Hedge Against Inflation

One of the unique advantages of real estate investing is its ability to act as a hedge against inflation. Inflation erodes the purchasing power of money, making it more expensive to buy goods and services over time. However, real estate tends to keep pace with or even outpace inflation, making it an effective way to preserve wealth.

Property values, like rental rates, generally increase during inflation periods. As the cost of living rises, the value of your real estate investments and the income generated from rental properties will likely rise; as a result, your retirement income keeps pace with inflation, preserving your purchasing power and living standards.

8.7 Real-Life Example: Building a Real Estate Portfolio

Consider the story of John and Emily, a couple who decided to invest in real estate in their early 40s as part of their retirement plan. They began by purchasing a duplex and living in one unit while renting out the other. The rental income helped cover their mortgage, saving them more money for future investments.

A few years later, John and Emily purchased a second property—a single-family home in a growing neighborhood. They hired a property management company to handle the day-to-day responsibilities, allowing them to focus on their careers and family. Over the next decade, they continued acquiring additional rental properties, each generating passive income and appreciating.

By the time they reached their late 50s, John and Emily owned five rental properties, each providing consistent monthly income. The rental income, combined with the appreciation of their properties, allowed them to retire comfortably, knowing they had multiple income streams to support their lifestyle. Their success resulted from careful planning, strategic investments, and a commitment to building a diversified real estate portfolio.

8.8 Risks and Challenges of Real Estate Investing

While real estate can be a powerful tool for building retirement wealth, it's essential to understand the risks and challenges involved:

Market Fluctuations: Real estate markets can be unpredictable, and property values can fluctuate based on economic conditions, interest rates, and local supply and demand. It's essential to be prepared for the possibility that your property may not appreciate as expected or may even lose value.

Vacancy and Tenant Issues: Rental properties are only profitable if paid tenants occupy them. Vacancies can lead to lost income, while problem tenants can cause property damage or fail to pay rent. Proper tenant screening and maintaining a reserve fund for unexpected expenses can help mitigate these risks.

Illiquidity: Real estate is considered an **illiquid** asset, meaning it can take time to sell a property if you need access to cash quickly. Unlike stocks or bonds, which can be sold with the click of a button, selling real estate can take time and involve significant transaction costs.

Maintenance and Management: Owning rental properties requires ongoing maintenance and management. If you're not prepared to handle these responsibilities, you may need to hire a property management company, which will reduce your net rental income.

8.9 Practical Tips for Getting Started in Real Estate Investing

If you're interested in using real estate to build wealth for retirement, here are some practical tips to help you get started:

Start Small: You don't need to buy a large apartment building to start investing in real estate. Consider starting with a single-family home or a duplex and learn the ropes without taking too much risk.

Educate Yourself: Real estate investing comes with a learning curve. Take the time to educate yourself on real estate finance, property management, and local market conditions. There are many books, online courses, and regional real estate investment groups that can help you build your knowledge.

Build a Strong Network: Successful real estate investors often rely on a network of professionals, including real estate agents, contractors, property managers, and attorneys. Building a solid network can help you find deals, manage properties, and navigate the challenges of real estate investing.

Run the Numbers: Before purchasing a property, it's crucial to **run the numbers** to ensure it will be a profitable investment. Consider purchase price, rental income, property taxes, insurance, maintenance costs, and vacancy rates. Ensure the property generates positive cash flow and meets your financial goals.

Consider Financing Options: Real estate investing often involves using leverage, or borrowed money, to finance the purchase of properties. While leverage can amplify your returns, it also comes with increased risk. Be sure to explore different financing options, including traditional mortgages, private lenders, and partnerships, to find the best fit for your situation.

Real estate investing can be a powerful tool for building wealth and generating income for retirement. Whether you invest in rental properties, REITs, or other types of real estate, the key is to approach it with a clear plan, a willingness to learn, and a commitment to managing your investments effectively.

By generating passive income, benefiting from property appreciation, and taking advantage of tax benefits, real estate can help you create a more secure and comfortable retirement. However, it's essential to be aware of the risks and challenges and mitigate them through careful planning, proper management, and diversification.

Howard Schultz –*"Risk more than others think is safe. Dream more than others think is practical."*

CHAPTER 9: ADDRESSING COMMON RETIREMENT FEARS AND MISCONCEPTIONS

Picture this: you've spent decades working hard, saving diligently, and dreaming of a retirement filled with relaxation and adventure. Yet, as you approach this new chapter, whispers of doubt and confusion cloud your vision. Retirement planning is fraught with myths and misconceptions that can derail even the most well-intentioned efforts. Let's unravel these myths, clarifying the path to a secure and fulfilling retirement. Many believe in the so-called "magic number" for retirement savings—a universal figure that promises security. In truth, this number varies widely based on your lifestyle and location. For instance, city living might require a bigger nest egg than a quiet rural life. Personal aspirations and health considerations further skew this figure. Instead of fixating on an arbitrary number, focus on crafting a personalized plan that reflects your unique needs. This approach ensures your savings align with your vision for retirement, providing peace of mind as you transition into this new phase.

9.1 Debunking Retirement Planning Myths

Investment risks often loom large in the minds of those nearing retirement. Fears of market downturns and losing hard-earned money can be paralyzing. It's important to understand that while stocks come with risks, they also offer growth opportunities. The key lies in the differentiation between short-term volatility and long-term trends. Markets fluctuate, but history shows they generally rise over time. Diversifying your portfolio can mitigate these risks, spreading potential losses across various assets. This strategy reduces exposure to individual market shifts and enhances your overall security. By focusing on long-term growth and maintaining a balanced portfolio, you can weather financial storms and capitalize on market recoveries.

Retirement age is another subject rife with misconceptions. The notion that 65 is the "right" age to retire is outdated and often misleading. This traditional benchmark arose when life expectancies were shorter and financial needs differed. Today, people live longer, healthier lives, and retirement is more a personal decision than a societal norm. Health, job satisfaction, and financial readiness are crucial in determining when to retire. Some may work longer to enhance their savings, while others prioritize leisure and family time. The right age is the one that aligns with your circumstances and goals, not a one-size-fits-all number imposed by convention.

Healthcare expenses in retirement can be a source of anxiety, often underestimated by those planning their golden years. With Medicare providing only partial coverage, retirees face out-of-pocket costs for premiums, deductibles, and co-payments. Long-term care expenses further complicate this picture. Many assume these costs will be minimal, but they often surprise retirees with their magnitude. Planning is essential to manage these expenses effectively. Consider supplemental insurance or long-term care policies to bridge gaps in coverage. By anticipating healthcare costs and incorporating them into your retirement plan, you can avoid unpleasant financial surprises and ensure you have the resources needed to maintain your well-being.

Interactive Element: Retirement Planning Reality Check

Consider using a Retirement Planning Reality Check to evaluate your understanding of these myths and misconceptions. This tool can help identify areas where your assumptions need adjustment, providing a clearer picture of your retirement readiness. Regularly revisiting this exercise ensures that your plans align with your evolving circumstances and goals.

9.2 Overcoming the Fear of Outliving Savings

Imagine the fear of outliving your savings as an ever-present shadow that looms over the prospect of retirement. This anxiety is common, but it can be managed with the right strategy. The cornerstone of this strategy is maintaining a sustainable withdrawal rate. The widely recognized 4% rule offers a guideline: it suggests withdrawing 4% of your retirement portfolio in the first year and adjusting that amount for inflation in subsequent years. This approach aims to preserve your savings over a 30-year retirement. However, it's not a one-size-fits-all solution. Some retirees might benefit from a more conservative rate, especially during economic downturns, while others might have room to adjust upward. It's about finding a balance that suits your unique circumstances and risk tolerance. Consider various withdrawal strategies, such as dynamic withdrawal, which adjusts based on market performance, to optimize your financial longevity.

For those seeking additional security, longevity insurance options provide a safety net. Deferred and longevity income annuities are designed to offer financial protection for extended lifespans. These products typically require an upfront payment in exchange for guaranteed income starting at a future date, often when you reach a certain age. With deferred income annuities, you purchase the annuity before retiring and begin receiving payments later, ensuring a steady income flow in your later years. On the other hand, longevity annuities kick in at an advanced age, such as 80 or 85, serving as a financial backstop in case you outlive your other savings. These options can be integrated into your retirement plan to provide peace of mind and a reliable income stream, especially if longevity runs in your family or if you worry about outlasting your assets.

Flexibility is vital in any retirement plan. Life is unpredictable, and your financial strategy should reflect that reality. You can preserve your savings and mitigate losses by adapting your spending plans during market downturns, such as tightening your budget during lean years or delaying large purchases until your financial outlook improves. Flexibility also extends to your broader financial strategy. Reassess your asset allocation regularly, ensuring it aligns with your risk tolerance and market conditions. A flexible approach allows you to navigate economic ebbs and flows, maintaining stability and security in retirement. It's about being prepared to pivot and adjust, ensuring your plan remains robust despite life's inevitable changes.

Continuous financial review is the linchpin of a successful retirement strategy. Annual financial check-ups offer a systematic way to assess your progress and make necessary adjustments. During these reviews, evaluate your withdrawal rate, investment performance, and financial goals. Are your savings on track to last through retirement? Are there changes in your personal life or the economy that warrant a shift in strategy? By regularly reviewing your plan, you stay informed and proactive, able to make adjustments before issues arise. This ongoing assessment ensures that your retirement plan evolves with you, adapting to new realities and maintaining its effectiveness over time. It's not just about setting a plan in motion; it's about nurturing and refining it throughout your retirement years.

To aid in this process, consider using a Retirement Income Planner. This tool can help you track your withdrawals, investment growth, and expenditures, clearly showing your financial health. By maintaining a comprehensive overview of your finances, you can make informed decisions and adjustments, ensuring your savings support your lifestyle and longevity.

9.3 Understanding Market Volatility and Its Impact

Financial markets are as unpredictable as the weather, with cycles of boom and bust that can leave even seasoned investors feeling seasick. Historically, markets have seen periods of both exuberant growth and sharp decline, each cycle shaping the financial landscape. Take the 1980s and 1990s bull markets, which brought unprecedented growth, followed by the dot-com bust and the 2008 financial crisis. These events underscore a critical truth: markets are inherently volatile. Yet, over the long term, they trend upward, driven by economic growth and innovation. This historical perspective is crucial for understanding the cyclical nature of markets. It emphasizes maintaining a long-term view rather than catching up in daily fluctuations and recognizing that temporary downturns can reduce anxiety and provide a more stable foundation for your investment strategy.

To navigate this volatility, you need a toolkit of strategies that can mitigate its impact on your financial health. Diversification across asset classes is a fundamental principle. By spreading investments across stocks, bonds, and alternative assets, you reduce the risk of any single investment dramatically affecting your portfolio. This approach allows you to tap into different growth opportunities while cushioning against the inevitable downturns in specific sectors. Another effective strategy is dollar-cost averaging, which involves investing a fixed amount at regular intervals regardless of market conditions. This method reduces the impact of short-term volatility by purchasing more shares when prices are low and fewer when they are high. Over time, this can lower the average cost per share and reduce the risk of making poorly timed investments. These strategies work together to smooth out the ride, allowing you to stay the course even when markets are rocky.

Emotional discipline is an often overlooked aspect of successful investing. When markets wobble, the instinctive reaction is to sell off assets in a panic. However, this can lock in losses and prevent you from benefiting from eventual recoveries. Instead, maintaining composure and focusing on your long-term goals is paramount. Avoiding panic selling requires a solid understanding of your investment strategy and confidence in your long-term plan. This mindset helps you make rational decisions rather than being swayed by the emotional rollercoaster of market swings. Staying calm and sticking to your plan is particularly important during downturns, as these periods can present opportunities to buy high-quality investments at reduced prices. By focusing on the bigger picture, you resist the urge to react impulsively, ensuring that your investments align with your goals.

Market volatility can significantly impact retirement income, mainly through the sequence of returns risk. This risk refers to the order in which investment returns occur, which can affect the sustainability of your withdrawals. In retirement, withdrawing funds during a market downturn can deplete your savings faster than anticipated. Therefore, it's crucial to implement a strategic withdrawal plan that accounts for market conditions. Establishing a cash reserve is one practical approach. By keeping a portion of your portfolio in cash or cash equivalents, you create a buffer that allows you to draw on these funds during market downturns, preserving your investments for future growth. This reserve provides liquidity, reducing the need to sell investments at a loss during market lows. Additionally, regularly reviewing and adjusting your asset allocation ensures that your portfolio remains aligned with your risk tolerance and financial goals, further protecting against volatility.

Visual Element: Volatility Impact Chart

Consider using a Volatility Impact Chart to visualize how different asset allocations respond to market fluctuations. This tool can illustrate the effects of diversification and the benefits of maintaining a cash reserve, helping you understand the practical implications of the strategies discussed. By providing a clear picture of potential outcomes, this chart aids in making informed decisions about managing market volatility in your retirement plan.

9.4 Relying on Social Security: Myths vs. Reality

Social Security is often a cornerstone of retirement discussions, yet its role needs to be more frequently understood. It's crucial to recognize that Social Security was designed to be something other than your sole source of income in retirement. Instead, it serves as a supplement intended to provide a foundation you can build with savings, investments, and, if possible, pensions. On average, Social Security benefits replace only about 37% of past earnings for retirees, making it clear that relying solely on these benefits would likely result in a significant income shortfall. Proper retirement planning involves integrating Social Security into a broader financial strategy, ensuring it complements other income streams. This approach provides a more comprehensive safety net and empowers you to maintain your desired lifestyle throughout retirement.

Concerns regarding the solvency of Social Security often stir unease among future retirees. Current projections suggest that, without legislative intervention, the Social Security Trust Fund may face depletion around 2035. However, benefits will remain. Instead, ongoing payroll taxes are expected to cover approximately 83% of scheduled benefits, according to current estimates. While this reduction could impact retirees, it's important to note that potential reforms should be discussed, which could address these shortfalls. Proposals range from increasing the payroll tax rate to lifting the cap on taxable earnings. Understanding these dynamics can help you make informed decisions about your retirement planning. Staying informed about policy changes and legislative updates is vital, as these could significantly impact your future benefits and financial security.

Maximizing your Social Security benefits involves strategic planning. One of the most effective strategies is timing your claim. While you can begin receiving benefits at 62, waiting until your full retirement age—typically between 66 and 67, depending on your birth year—will result in larger monthly payments. The reward is even more significant for those who can delay benefits until age 70, with an increase of approximately 8% per year for each year you defer past full retirement age. Consider your health, financial needs, and employment situation when deciding when to claim benefits.

Additionally, spousal benefits present another opportunity for optimization. If you're married, you may be eligible to claim benefits based on your spouse's earnings record, which can be beneficial if their earnings are significantly higher than yours. Understanding these options allows you to tailor your strategy to maximize your household's benefits, contributing to a more stable retirement income.

Misunderstandings about eligibility and benefit amounts can lead to misguided expectations. Many falsely believe that simply reaching a certain age guarantees full benefits. In reality, the criteria for full retirement age vary, and your benefit amount depends on your earnings history and the age at which you start receiving benefits. The Social Security Administration calculates your benefit based on your highest 35 years of earnings, adjusted for inflation. Therefore, if you have fewer than 35 years of earnings, zeros are averaged in, potentially lowering your benefit.

Additionally, your benefits can be reduced if you continue to work while receiving Social Security before reaching full retirement age. For example, in 2024, you lose $1 in benefits for every $2 earned above $21,240. These nuances highlight the importance of understanding how your benefits are calculated. By grasping these details, you can make more informed choices, ensuring you optimize your Social Security benefits in alignment with your overall retirement plan.

9.5 The Emotional Transition to Retirement

Retirement is more than a financial change; it's a profound shift in how you perceive yourself and your place in the world. As you leave the structured work environment behind, you might grapple with questions of identity and purpose. Your career may have been a significant part of who you are, providing income and a sense of belonging and achievement. It's common to experience feelings of loss or anxiety as you adjust to new rhythms. The key is recognizing these emotions and giving them the space they deserve. Reflect on what you value most outside of your professional life. Consider the hobbies, passions, and interests that have always intrigued you but perhaps took a backseat during your working years. There's no better time than right now to redefine what gives your life meaning and to explore new avenues of fulfillment. By embracing this opportunity, you can craft a retirement that resonates with your aspirations and values.

Staying active and engaged is crucial to maintaining a vibrant and fulfilling retirement lifestyle. You now have the chance to delve into hobbies or interests you only had time to pursue partially. Whether painting, gardening, or learning a new language, engaging in activities stimulating your mind and body can be incredibly rewarding. These pursuits enrich your life and provide a structure to ease the transition from a busy work schedule to a more flexible routine. Volunteering is another excellent way to stay involved and contribute to your community. It offers a sense of purpose and connection, allowing you to share your skills and experience with others. Community involvement can take many forms, from mentoring young people to participating in local environmental projects. By staying active and engaged, you maintain a sense of purpose and fulfillment, which is vital for your overall well-being in retirement.

Social connections are the glue that holds our lives together, providing support, companionship, and joy. As you transition into retirement, you must nurture your existing relationships and build new ones. Without the daily interactions that work provides, your social circle might shrink. Be proactive in maintaining connections with friends and family. Arrange regular get-togethers or join groups that align with your interests. Participating in group activities, such as clubs or classes, can introduce you to new people and expand your network. These connections offer emotional support and can help stave off feelings of loneliness or isolation. A strong social network enhances your quality of life and provides a buffer against retirement's challenges.

Retirement can also bring potential mental health challenges that need to be addressed. It's essential to be aware of the signs of depression or anxiety, such as persistent sadness, loss of interest in activities you once enjoyed, or feelings of hopelessness. These issues are not uncommon and can affect anyone during significant life transitions. Early recognition of these signs can help you seek timely support. Don't hesitate to reach out to mental health professionals if you find yourself struggling. They can offer valuable tools and strategies to help you navigate these challenges. Additionally, consider engaging in activities that promote mental wellness, such as mindfulness practices or regular exercise. Taking care of your mental health is as important as managing your physical health, ensuring a well-rounded and fulfilling retirement.

The emotional transition into retirement is a multifaceted experience that requires attention and care. You can navigate this change with confidence and joy by embracing new interests, maintaining social connections, and prioritizing mental health. This chapter's insights are meant to equip you with the understanding and tools needed to thrive in this new phase of life, setting the stage for exploring how to maintain a sustainable and rewarding lifestyle in retirement.

Jack Welch *—"Before you are a leader, success is all about growing yourself. When you become a leader, success is all about growing others."*

CHAPTER 10: EMBRACING A HOLISTIC RETIREMENT LIFESTYLE

Imagine waking up each day with a renewed sense of purpose, where your mornings are filled with activities that invigorate your body and mind. The above statement is how a holistic retirement lifestyle that harmonizes physical health, mental well-being, and personal fulfillment would look like. As you transition into this new chapter, you must focus on nurturing your entire self. Retirement isn't merely about financial security; it's about embracing a lifestyle that enriches every aspect of your being. By prioritizing health and wellness, you can ensure your retirement years are long, vibrant, and fulfilling.

10.1 Planning for Health and Wellness in Retirement

Physical activity is a cornerstone of a fulfilling retirement. Regular exercise promotes longevity and enhances your quality of life by boosting your mood, improving sleep, and reducing the risk of chronic diseases. Developing a personalized exercise regimen tailored to your interests and abilities is key. Consider low-impact activities like swimming or yoga, which are gentle on the joints yet effective in building strength and flexibility. These exercises enhance physical fitness and offer mental relaxation, helping to alleviate stress and anxiety. Joining local fitness groups or classes can provide additional motivation and social interaction, making exercise an enjoyable part of your routine. Integrating physical activity into your daily life supports physical and social well-being, whether a morning walk with friends or a community yoga session.

Nutrition plays an equally vital role in maintaining health as you age. A balanced diet rich in whole foods—fruits, vegetables, whole grains, lean proteins, and healthy fats—supports your body's changing needs and helps prevent malnutrition. Meal planning can simplify healthy eating, ensuring you have nutritious meals ready without the stress of deciding what to eat daily. Consulting with a nutritionist can offer personalized advice, helping you address specific dietary needs or health concerns. They can guide you in managing weight, preventing chronic diseases, and maintaining energy levels. Keeping your diet diverse and colorful ensures you receive a wide range of nutrients and keeps your meals appealing and enjoyable. This eating approach supports your physical health and enhances your overall well-being, allowing you to savor the pleasures of life with vitality.

Managing stress is crucial in retirement, as it can impact physical and mental health. Practicing mindfulness and meditation are effective techniques for enhancing mental well-being. These practices encourage living in the moment, reducing worry about the future and regret about the past. Simple mindfulness exercises, like focused breathing and non-judgemental observing of your feelings, can be done anywhere and anytime. Meditation, even for just a few minutes daily, can reduce stress and improve emotional health. Engaging in relaxation techniques like deep breathing or progressive muscle relaxation can also alleviate tension and promote a sense of calm. By incorporating these practices into your routine, you cultivate resilience against life's challenges, fostering a peaceful and balanced state of mind.

Regular health check-ups are an integral part of maintaining well-being in retirement. Scheduling routine medical appointments helps prevent and manage health issues before they become significant concerns. Create a medical appointment schedule that includes regular visits to your primary care physician and necessary screenings such as blood pressure checks, cholesterol tests, and cancer screenings. Keeping track of vaccinations and preventive screenings protects you against preventable diseases. Emphasize the importance of open communication with your healthcare providers, sharing any concerns or symptoms you may experience. This proactive approach to healthcare enables you to maintain your independence and enjoy a healthy, active lifestyle well into your later years.

Interactive Element: Wellness Journal

Consider maintaining a Wellness Journal to track your physical activity, nutrition, and stress management practices. Record your daily exercise routines, meals, and reflections on your mental well-being. Note any changes in your health or mood, and set wellness goals for yourself, such as trying a new exercise class or incorporating more vegetables into your diet. This journal is a personal accountability tool, helping you stay committed to your health and wellness journey. As you document your progress, you'll gain insights into what works best for you, allowing you to make informed decisions about your lifestyle choices.

10.2 Pursuing Passions: Travel and Hobbies

Imagine opening your eyes to a sunrise in a city you've always dreamed of visiting or feeling the exhilaration of trying a new hobby that sparks joy. Retirement offers a chance to explore passions that work commitments may have sidelined. Travel is a powerful way to ignite your sense of adventure and curiosity. Start by crafting a travel bucket list that reflects your interests, whether exploring historical sites, relaxing on a beach, or experiencing local cultures. Consider group travel opportunities for older adults, providing camaraderie and shared experiences. These trips can be enriching as you connect with others who share your enthusiasm. Budgeting wisely for travel expenses ensures you enjoy these adventures without financial stress. Allocate funds specifically for travel, and look for deals or packages that offer savings, allowing you to focus on the experience, not the cost.

Creative pursuits can be a fulfilling part of retirement, offering new ways to express yourself and stay mentally stimulated. Delve into artistic hobbies such as painting, photography, or music—activities that nurture the soul and provide satisfaction. These creative outlets allow you to explore your imagination and hone skills that bring joy and relaxation. Setting up a home studio or workshop can create a dedicated space for these activities, allowing you to explore creativity without distractions. This space becomes a personal sanctuary where you can lose yourself in the process of creating, leaving stress and worries behind. Classes in these areas, whether online or in person, offer structured learning and the opportunity to meet others with similar interests. Engaging in these activities enhances your artistic abilities and creates a sense of accomplishment and purpose.

The great outdoors beckons with opportunities to develop skills that enhance physical health and enjoyment. Gardening connects you with nature while providing a sense of pride and fulfillment. Watching plants grow and thrive under your care can be immensely rewarding, offering beauty and tranquility to your surroundings. Bird watching is another hobby that invites patience and observation, deepening your appreciation for wildlife and the environment. For those seeking more active pursuits, joining hiking or cycling clubs can provide physical exercise and social interaction. These clubs often organize outings, introducing you to new trails and scenic locations, adding excitement and variety to your routine. The camaraderie of shared interests fosters friendships, providing motivation and encouragement to stay active and engaged.

Volunteering offers a meaningful way to pursue passions while contributing to the community. For example, participating in local conservation projects allows you to support environmental efforts and make a tangible difference. Planting trees, cleaning up local parks, or restoring natural habitats benefit the environment and your sense of purpose. Volunteering at schools or community centers offers another avenue for engagement through tutoring, mentoring, or organizing events. These roles can be incredibly rewarding, allowing you to share your knowledge and experience with others and fostering connections across generations. The impact of volunteering extends beyond the immediate benefits; it strengthens community ties and enriches your own life by providing opportunities to learn and grow.

As you embrace these pursuits, consider how they align with your interests and lifestyle. Each activity uniquely enriches your daily life, providing joy, fulfillment, and lasting memories. Whether exploring the world, creating art, engaging with nature, or giving back to the community, pursuing these passions ensures that your retirement years are vibrant and meaningful. The possibilities are endless, limited only by your imagination and willingness to explore new horizons.

10.3 The Role of Lifelong Learning and Personal Growth

As you transition into retirement, the opportunity to engage in continuous education becomes an enticing prospect. It's a chance to stretch your mind, explore new interests, and keep your cognitive faculties sharp. Enrolling in online courses or community college classes offers a flexible way to delve into subjects that pique your curiosity or enhance your expertise. Whether exploring the intricacies of digital photography, understanding the basics of a new language, or diving into a historical era that fascinated you in your youth, these learning opportunities provide a structured yet adaptable approach to acquiring knowledge. Workshops and seminars also present avenues to immerse yourself in topics of interest, often bringing together like-minded individuals who share your quest for learning. This environment stimulates intellectual growth and fosters community, where you can exchange ideas and insights with peers.

Cultivating new skills and hobbies during retirement is not just about filling time; it's about enriching your life with experiences that bring satisfaction and joy. Learning a new language, for instance, opens doors to different cultures and perspectives, enhancing your travel experiences and personal interactions. It challenges your brain, keeping it active and engaged. Similarly, exploring digital literacy and technology can be both practical and rewarding. In an increasingly digital world, understanding how to navigate new technologies can enhance your daily life, keeping you connected and informed. Whether mastering a new software program or understanding the nuances of social media platforms, these skills ensure you remain engaged with the modern world, fostering a sense of accomplishment and relevance.

Setting personal development goals is a powerful way to align your actions with your values and interests. Begin by creating an individual development plan that outlines what you wish to achieve in various aspects of your life, whether intellectual, emotional, or creative. This plan acts as a roadmap, guiding you toward meaningful accomplishments. As you progress, track your achievements and celebrate milestones along the way. These small or grand celebrations reinforce your commitment to personal growth, motivating you to strive for improvement. Tracking progress also helps identify areas where you may need to adjust your efforts or explore new avenues, ensuring your development journey remains dynamic and fulfilling. By consistently setting and achieving goals, you cultivate a sense of purpose and direction, enhancing your overall quality of life.

Embracing creative expression and innovation invites you to challenge your abilities and explore uncharted territories of personal potential. Writing memoirs or starting a blog allows you to document your experiences, thoughts, and insights, creating a legacy of wisdom and reflection that others can learn from. This creative endeavor sharpens your writing skills and encourages introspection and emotional awareness. Engaging in DIY projects or crafts offers another outlet for creativity, allowing you to transform ideas into tangible results. Whether it's building furniture, crafting a unique piece of jewelry, or designing a garden landscape, these projects stimulate the mind and provide a sense of achievement. They encourage problem-solving, innovation, and the satisfaction of creating something with your hands. These activities are not just hobbies; they are transformative experiences that enrich your life and broaden your horizons, encouraging continual growth and exploration.

As you explore the possibilities of lifelong learning and personal growth, consider how these pursuits can enhance your retirement. Each new skill, hobby, or project adds a layer of richness to your daily routine, offering opportunities for reflection, connection, and joy. Pursuing knowledge and creative expression, you find fulfillment and a deeper understanding of yourself and the world around you.

10.4 Maintaining Social Connections and Community Involvement

The bonds we share with loved ones become even more precious in retirement. Strengthening family relationships nurtures the heart and creates cherished memories that last a lifetime. Consider organizing regular family gatherings or reunions. These events don't need to be elaborate; they can be simple get-togethers that bring everyone together. The goal is to foster a sense of unity and belonging. Engaging in multi-generational activities, such as family game nights or storytelling sessions, can bridge the gap between young and old, offering a platform for sharing stories and experiences. These activities strengthen familial bonds and instill a sense of history and tradition in younger family members. By prioritizing family, you ensure these relationships remain strong and meaningful throughout retirement.

Friendships, too, play a vital role in enriching your life. As you step away from the workplace, maintaining and building new friendships can provide support and joy. Joining social clubs or interest groups is an excellent way to meet like-minded individuals. Whether it's a book club, gardening group, or a local sports team, these gatherings offer opportunities to connect with others who share your passions. They provide a sense of community, where friendships can blossom naturally. Hosting social events or meetings at your home can also be a delightful way to deepen existing friendships and forge new ones. These occasions create an inviting atmosphere where laughter and conversation flow easily, strengthening the connections that enhance your life. By cultivating friendships, you develop a network of support and companionship that enriches your retirement experience.

Community involvement can also provide a fulfilling dimension to your retirement. Participating in community projects and events fosters a sense of belonging and purpose. Volunteering for local charities or organizations allows you to contribute your skills and time to causes you care about. Whether mentoring young students, organizing charity events, or helping at a local food bank, your involvement makes a difference. Attending community festivals or fairs is another way to engage with your surroundings. These events offer a chance to meet new people, celebrate local culture, and enjoy the lively atmosphere. By immersing yourself in community activities, you not only enhance your social life but also contribute to the vibrancy and well-being of your community. This engagement provides a sense of fulfillment and connection, knowing your efforts positively impact those around you.

In today's digital age, technology offers a powerful tool for maintaining social connections. Social media platforms can help you stay in touch with family and friends, regardless of distance. These platforms provide a window into the lives of loved ones, allowing you to share moments, exchange messages, and even engage in video calls. Participating in online forums or virtual meetups can also expand your social circles. These virtual communities unite people from various backgrounds and interests, providing a platform for sharing ideas and discussing everyday topics. Whether it's a forum dedicated to a hobby you love or a virtual book club, these interactions foster a sense of community and connection. By leveraging technology, you can overcome geographical barriers and maintain meaningful relationships, ensuring you remain connected and engaged no matter where life takes you.

As you embrace these facets of social connection and community involvement, consider how they contribute to your well-being. Solid relationships and community ties enrich your life, providing joy, support, and a sense of purpose. Each interaction with family, friends, or community members adds depth and meaning to your days. By nurturing these connections, you create a fulfilling and profoundly rewarding retirement. These efforts lead to a life surrounded by love and community, enhancing every moment of your retirement.

Richard Branson *–"Business opportunities are like buses; there's always another one coming."*

CHAPTER 11: FUTURE-PROOFING YOUR RETIREMENT PLAN

Picture this: the comfortable retirement you've envisioned, suddenly shaken by a volatile economy. The recent past has taught us that economic shifts can be swift and unsettling. Yet, you can navigate these changes with foresight and flexibility and secure your retirement future. This chapter provides essential strategies to adapt your plans, ensuring resilience in economic uncertainty.

11.1 Adapting to Economic Changes

Understanding global economic trends is crucial for personal financial strategies. Economic shifts can influence everything from interest rates to inflation, impacting your retirement nest egg. For instance, fluctuations in global markets can affect the value of your investments, altering your portfolio's performance. Economic indicators like GDP growth rates and unemployment figures should be considered to navigate these changes. These indicators provide insights into the broader economic climate, helping you anticipate potential impacts on your investments and adjust your strategies accordingly.

Inflation and deflation are two economic forces that can significantly affect your retirement savings. Inflation erodes purchasing power, while deflation can lead to economic stagnation. To manage inflation, consider adjusting your portfolio allocations. Increasing your exposure to stocks can provide growth potential that outpaces inflation, while incorporating commodities like gold can serve as a hedge. Maintaining a portion of your portfolio in cash or short-term bonds can provide stability for deflation. Additionally, hedging against currency fluctuations with investments in foreign assets can protect your portfolio from adverse shifts in exchange rates.

Interest rate changes also play a pivotal role in retirement planning. Rising rates can increase income from fixed-income investments, benefiting retirees on a fixed income. However, they can also depress bond prices, leading to losses in bond-heavy portfolios. To adapt, consider diversifying your fixed-income investments with short- and long-term bonds. Additionally, refinancing existing debts with low rates can reduce interest payments, freeing up more funds for savings or investment. Monitoring rate trends helps ensure your portfolio remains aligned with the current economic environment.

Economic downturns are inevitable, and preparing for them is essential. Building a cash reserve can provide a buffer during turbulent times, allowing you to meet expenses without selling investments at a loss. Reducing discretionary spending can bolster savings, providing additional security during economic instability. Trimming non-essential costs can increase your savings rate, enhancing your financial resilience. This proactive approach ensures financial stability, even when faced with unexpected economic challenges.

Textual Element: Economic Resilience Checklist

Use an Economic Resilience Checklist to review and adjust your financial strategies periodically. This tool can help you assess your current economic exposure, identify potential vulnerabilities, and implement necessary adjustments to safeguard your retirement plan. Regularly updating this checklist ensures your strategies remain effective, providing peace of mind as you navigate the complexities of the global economy.

11.2 Adjusting Plans for Personal Life Transitions

Life has a way of surprising us, and these changes often come with financial implications that require careful consideration. Marriage or divorce can dramatically alter your financial landscape. When you marry, assets merge, and financial goals often shift to accommodate shared dreams and responsibilities. Revisiting your retirement plan is crucial, as well as ensuring that it reflects your new joint financial picture. Conversely, divorce can divide assets and require reevaluating your retirement strategy. It may mean reassessing your financial goals and adjusting your savings plan to ensure you remain on track for a secure future. The birth of grandchildren adds another layer to your family dynamics. It might inspire new financial goals, such as contributing to educational savings plans or adjusting your estate planning to include them in your legacy.

Health-related changes can be unpredictable, yet they significantly affect your retirement planning. As health needs evolve, you may need to adjust your healthcare coverage; for instance, increasing your health savings account contributions or exploring supplemental insurance to cover gaps in Medicare. Planning for potential long-term care needs is also essential. Consider setting aside funds or investing in long-term care insurance to protect your assets from being depleted by unforeseen medical expenses. These steps ensure your health needs are met without compromising your financial security.

Relocation or downsizing presents another critical transition. Whether moving to a new city for a change of scenery or downsizing to reduce expenses, careful financial planning is required. Calculate the costs and benefits of relocating, considering factors like housing prices, cost of living, and proximity to family and healthcare. Budget for moving expenses and any fees associated with settling into a new home, such as renovations or new furnishings. Downsizing can free up equity and reduce maintenance costs, providing additional funds to bolster your retirement savings.

Changes in employment status also necessitate adjustments. Transitioning to part-time work or consulting roles can supplement your retirement income while allowing flexibility. If you own a business, navigating retirement while managing it requires a plan to delegate responsibilities or gradually transition out of your role.

11.3 Leveraging Technology in Retirement Planning

In today's fast-paced digital world, technology has become an invaluable ally in managing your retirement planning. Financial planning software stands out for its ability to streamline and organize complex financial data. These tools offer features like real-time tracking of investments and expenses, providing a clear picture of your financial health. With user-friYoungs goals, monitor cash flow and predict future economic scenarios. This digital, user-friendly interface helps you make informed decisions, ensuring your retirement plan remains robust and adaptable to change. By integrating these tools into your routine, you understand where you stand and what adjustments are necessary to keep your retirement goals on track.

Staying informed about financial news and trends is another critical aspect of leveraging technology. Subscribing to financial news platforms and alerts keeps you updated on market changes, economic forecasts, and investment opportunities. These insights can be pivotal in making timely adjustments to your portfolio. Additionally, joining online financial communities provides a platform for exchanging ideas and gaining insights from fellow investors. These communities often share real-time experiences and strategies, offering diverse perspectives that can enrich your understanding and approach to financial planning. Engaging with these resources empowers you to stay ahead of the curve, making informed decisions that align with your financial objectives.

Digital banking and investment platforms have revolutionized how we manage our finances. Online banking offers convenience and efficiency, allowing you to monitor accounts, transfer funds, and pay bills from home. Mobile apps extend this convenience to on-the-go management, ensuring you control your finances.

Furthermore, robo-advisors provide automated investment management, using algorithms to build and manage a diversified portfolio tailored to your risk tolerance and goals. These platforms offer low-cost solutions and take the guesswork out of investing, making them an attractive option for those seeking a hands-off approach to wealth management.

As you embrace digital solutions, safeguarding your online financial transactions becomes paramount. Implementing strong cybersecurity measures, such as using complex passwords and enabling two-factor authentication, protects your data from potential threats. Using secure and reputable financial platforms is vital, ensuring your information is encrypted and protected. Staying vigilant about cybersecurity safeguards your assets and provides peace of mind, allowing you to focus on building a secure financial future.

11.4 Continuous Learning and Financial Education

Lifelong financial education is more than a buzzword; it's a necessary commitment to keeping your financial strategies sharp and adaptive. The financial landscape constantly evolves, with new products, services, and regulations emerging regularly. Immersing yourself in financial workshops and seminars can provide valuable insights and updates. These events offer access to experts who can distill complex topics into actionable advice. Online courses and webinars expand this learning, offering flexibility and various topics from investment basics to advanced financial methodologies. Embracing these educational opportunities ensures you remain informed and capable of making sound financial decisions.

Exploring new financial products and services is crucial for maintaining a diversified and robust portfolio. Today's investment world offers many emerging vehicles, from exchange-traded funds (ETFs) tailored to specific sectors to innovative savings accounts providing higher returns. Understanding blockchain and cryptocurrencies is also becoming increasingly relevant. While still volatile, these technologies present opportunities and risks that require careful consideration. By staying informed, you can better evaluate these options and understand their implications and potential roles in your financial strategy. This proactive approach helps you anticipate market shifts and capitalize on new opportunities.

Engaging with financial experts and advisors is invaluable. These professionals provide personalized guidance, helping navigate complex financial terrain. Building a relationship with a certified financial planner can offer reassurance, especially during uncertain times. Whether considering a significant investment or rethinking your retirement strategy, their expertise can illuminate paths you need help to see. Consulting specialists for niche financial advice, such as tax planning or estate management, can also refine your strategies, enhancing efficiency and effectiveness.

Participating in peer learning opportunities enriches your financial knowledge through shared experiences. Investment clubs and discussion forums offer platforms to exchange ideas and strategies with others who share your interests. These groups provide diverse perspectives, often revealing insights that challenge conventional thinking. Book clubs focusing on financial literature can deepen your understanding and spark new ideas. Engaging in these communities fosters an environment of learning and support, reinforcing the notion that financial education is a collaborative, ongoing process.

11.5 Building Resilience in Uncertain Times

Cultivating a resilient financial mindset is crucial in today's unpredictable economic landscape. One can start by adopting a long-term perspective, recognizing that markets will fluctuate but generally trend upward over time. Patience and discipline are key. Rather than reacting impulsively to short-term market changes, stay committed to your investment strategy. It is vital to hold steady during downturns and the foresight not to chase overly risky ventures during booms. By focusing on long-term goals, you can confidently weather the ebbs and flows of financial markets.

Establishing financial safety nets is another pillar of resilience. One practical approach is to build a diversified income strategy., which may include income from investments, part-time work, or rental properties, ensuring you're not overly dependent on a single source. Additionally, setting up emergency savings accounts is vital. These funds should be easily accessible and cover three to six months of living expenses, providing a buffer against unforeseen events such as job loss or sudden medical expenses. These safety nets enhance your ability to navigate financial uncertainties without derailing your broader retirement plans.

Risk management strategies form the backbone of a secure financial plan. Insurance is crucial, offering protection against potential health and property-related losses. Comprehensive health and homeowners or renters insurance can safeguard your assets and prevent significant financial setbacks. Additionally, hedging against investment risks is wise and can easily be achieved by diversifying your portfolio across various asset classes and geographies, reducing exposure to sector-specific downturns. By proactively managing risk, you can protect your wealth from unforeseen events or market shifts, ensuring your financial security remains intact.

Flexibility in financial planning must be balanced. As life circumstances and economic conditions change, so should your financial plans. Adapting your budget and spending habits as needed allows you to accommodate new priorities or respond to financial challenges. Regularly revisiting your financial goals ensures they remain relevant and achievable. Adjust your priorities and strategies to align with your current situation and aspirations.

This dynamic approach to planning fosters resilience, equipping you to handle whatever challenges life may present.

11.6 Monitoring and Revisiting Your Retirement Plan

Regular financial check-ups are vital in the ever-changing finance landscape to ensure your retirement plan aligns with your goals. Think of it as a health check-up for your finances. Schedule annual reviews with your financial advisor to analyze your current situation and adjust your strategy. These consultations offer a chance to reflect on any shifts in your financial circumstances, such as income changes or unexpected expenses, and recalibrate your plan accordingly. By staying proactive, you maintain control over your financial trajectory, ensuring your retirement objectives remain within reach.

Tracking progress toward your retirement goals requires setting clear benchmarks and milestones. And no, tracking progress isn't just about watching numbers grow; it's about understanding how each financial decision impacts your overall plan. Establish measurable targets, whether reaching a specific savings amount or achieving a desired investment return. Regularly assess your progress against these benchmarks, and be prepared to adjust your tactics if you need to catch up. This dynamic approach keeps you on course, allowing for strategic modifications that enhance your financial security and confidence.

Updating your retirement plan to reflect personal changes is crucial as life unfolds. Family dynamics, such as changes in marital status or the addition of dependents, can significantly impact your financial priorities. Revising your estate plan to accommodate these shifts ensures your assets are distributed according to your current wishes. Similarly, modifying your investment strategy becomes necessary as your risk tolerance evolves with age or circumstances.

This adaptability allows your retirement plan to grow with you, providing a stable foundation for your future.

Leverage technology for efficient plan monitoring and adjustments. Financial dashboard tools offer a comprehensive overview of your assets, liabilities, and progress toward your goals. These platforms provide alerts and notifications for timely decision-making, helping you stay informed of significant market movements or personal financial milestones. By integrating these digital resources, you streamline the management of your retirement plan, making it easier to implement changes and maintain alignment with your objectives. This proactive approach empowers you to easily navigate the complexities of retirement planning, ensuring your financial future is secure and well-managed.

11.7 Innovative Tools for Retirement Planning

Exploring the landscape of emerging technologies reveals how they are reshaping the way we approach retirement planning. Artificial intelligence (AI) stands at the forefront, offering personalized financial advice that was once the realm of human advisors alone. AI analyzes vast data, providing insights tailored to your unique financial situation and goals. This technology enhances decision-making, helping you optimize investments and manage risks more effectively. Meanwhile, blockchain technology promises secure transactions and data integrity. By decentralizing data storage, blockchain reduces the risk of fraud, ensuring that your financial information remains safe and transparent. This technology can potentially revolutionize how we manage and protect our financial assets.

Utilizing retirement planning calculators can demystify the complexities of preparing for the future. These tools are invaluable for estimating retirement needs, offering projections for Social Security benefits, and calculating the savings required to maintain your desired lifestyle. You gain a clearer picture of your financial trajectory by inputting variables like age, income, and expenses. Calculators can also assist in determining optimal withdrawal strategies, ensuring that your savings last throughout your retirement years. This clarity empowers you to set realistic goals and track progress, providing confidence and direction in your planning efforts.

Virtual financial planning platforms have become indispensable, offering conveniences that traditional methods lack. You receive expert guidance through virtual meetings with financial advisors without needing face-to-face appointments. These platforms facilitate real-time collaboration, allowing you to adjust strategies based on immediate feedback. Online portfolio management systems provide a comprehensive overview of your investments, offering insights into performance and potential areas for improvement. This accessibility ensures that your financial plan remains aligned with your goals, adapting to changes in market conditions or personal circumstances.

It's a good idea to embrace financial apps for budgeting, saving, or streamlining your financial management. Budget tracking apps monitor daily expenses, helping you stay on track and identify areas for cost-cutting. Meanwhile, savings apps with automatic round-up features encourage consistent saving, rounding up purchases to the nearest dollar and transferring the difference to savings. This passive approach to saving can accumulate significant funds over time, providing a financial cushion for the future. These apps foster a disciplined approach to money management, making it easier to achieve your financial objectives without constant vigilance.

11.8 Inspiring Success Stories and Lessons Learned

Consider the story of Sarah, a nurse who meticulously planned her retirement over three decades. She diversified her investments early, balancing stocks with bonds, and incorporated real estate into her portfolio. By her late fifties, Sarah was financially secure and had the freedom to pursue her passion for painting full-time. Her success exemplifies the power of thoughtful, disciplined planning. Meanwhile, an engineer, John, underestimated healthcare costs and found his savings dwindling faster than anticipated. Learning from this, he adjusted his budget, sought supplemental insurance, and managed to stabilize his finances. These stories highlight the diverse paths to financial independence, showcasing triumphs and challenges.

Mistakes, while often costly, provide valuable lessons. Many retirees falter by overspending in their early retirement years, lured by the newfound freedom. They indulge in lavish vacations or expensive hobbies without considering long-term consequences. Impulsive indulgence can lead to financial strain later in life. Learning from these missteps, a prudent retiree might enjoy traveling but within a budget that safeguards future stability. Healthcare, another overlooked expense, often exceeds expectations. Failing to account for rising medical costs can derail even the best-laid plans. Addressing this involves factoring realistic healthcare expenses into retirement budgets and considering insurance options to mitigate financial risks.

Resilience shines through in stories of retirees who have overcome significant financial setbacks. Take the example of Maria, who faced unexpected expenses due to a market downturn. She navigated these challenges gracefully by adjusting her lifestyle and tapping into emergency savings. Her adaptability ensured she maintained a comfortable retirement without compromising her long-term goals. Similarly, Robert pursued an unconventional path by starting a small bakery post-retirement and using his passion to generate income and fulfillment. These narratives demonstrate the strength of adaptability and persistence in the face of adversity.

Diverse perspectives enrich our understanding of retirement. From cultural backgrounds that emphasize communal living to those that prioritize individual independence, each approach offers unique insights. Consider Amanda, who retired early to travel the world on a shoestring budget, immersing herself in different cultures. Her story reminds us that retirement isn't a one-size-fits-all journey but a personal experience shaped by individual values and choices.

11.9 Empowering the Next Generation in Financial Independence

Teaching financial literacy to younger generations is critical for their future success. It starts with the basics, such as budgeting and saving, which lay the groundwork for sound financial habits. Encourage them to set aside a portion of any income—even if it's just from an allowance or part-time job—into savings. This practice teaches discipline and the value of delayed gratification. Introduce investment principles early, explaining the power of compound interest and the benefits of starting young. Understanding these concepts allows them to make informed decisions and avoid common financial pitfalls. This knowledge empowers them to take charge of their financial futures confidently.

Involving your family in financial discussions cultivates an environment of openness and learning. Regular family meetings to discuss financial priorities can demystify money management and make it a shared responsibility. Engage children in conversations about estate planning, explaining how today's decisions affect future generations. This involvement fosters a sense of ownership and responsibility, encouraging them to think critically about their financial goals and the legacy they wish to build. Making financial discussions a regular part of family life creates a supportive atmosphere where questions are welcomed and learning is continuous.

Leading by example is one of the most effective ways to instill financial responsibility in the next generation. Demonstrate prudent financial behavior in your daily life, whether budgeting for groceries, saving for a vacation, or investing in a retirement account. Share personal experiences and lessons learned to illustrate the real-world impact of financial decisions. These stories provide valuable insights and serve as a powerful teaching tool. By modeling responsible financial practices, you inspire others to adopt similar habits, creating a ripple effect beyond your immediate family.

Building intergenerational wealth requires strategic planning and a focus on education and entrepreneurship. Establishing family trusts can protect assets and ensure they are passed down according to your wishes. Encourage entrepreneurial endeavors, supporting education and skill development to prepare them for future challenges. This approach secures financial resources and instills a mindset of innovation and resilience. By prioritizing long-term wealth-building strategies, you provide a foundation that empowers future generations to thrive financially and personally.

In conclusion, empowering the next generation with financial literacy and involving them in meaningful discussions lays the groundwork for a legacy of prosperity and informed decision-making. This approach ensures that financial wisdom and resources are effectively transferred, equipping them with the tools necessary to navigate their financial futures with confidence and foresight.

Keeping the Game Alive

Now that you have the tools to plan your dream retirement, it's time to share what you've learned and help others take the first step toward their future.

By leaving your honest opinion of *The Retirement Planning Accelerator* on Amazon, you'll guide others—just like you—who are searching for clarity and confidence in their retirement journey.

Your review can be the light that points them toward the information they need to build their future and keeps the momentum of retirement planning alive for everyone.

Thank you for being part of this mission. Retirement planning stays alive when we share our knowledge, and by leaving a review, you're helping me pass it forward to those who need it most.

>>> [Click here to leave your review on Amazon.](#)

Thank you for making a difference,
Jon J. McKenzie
Author of *The Retirement Planning Accelerator*

CONCLUSION

As you reach the end of this journey through retirement planning, it's essential to reflect on the path we've navigated together. From laying the groundwork of financial literacy to refining investment strategies, healthcare planning, tax considerations, and estate planning, each chapter has been a building block in constructing a robust and secure future. This book aims to provide a comprehensive view of retirement planning, encouraging a proactive approach encompassing all aspects of financial well-being.

Throughout the chapters, we've explored crucial concepts like conducting thorough financial audits to assess your current position. Crafting personalized savings plans is vital to ensuring financial security. Balancing debt and savings is another essential skill, as is understanding the intricate dance of investments. We've delved into healthcare cost estimation to prepare for unforeseen medical expenses and explored tax strategies to optimize savings and income. Deciding your ideal retirement age and building a sustainable income stream are pivotal steps in your journey. Lastly, estate planning ensures your legacy reflects your values and supports those you care about.

Taking away key lessons from these pages, remember that retirement planning is not a one-time task. It's a lifelong journey requiring continuous adaptation and learning. Proactive planning is your best ally, and diversification of investments is a powerful tool. Preparing for healthcare costs and adopting tax-efficient strategies are crucial elements of a successful plan. These efforts ensure you're ready for the future you envision.

Now, with knowledge in hand, it's time to act. Begin by conducting a personal financial audit. Set clear savings and investment goals. Engage with financial professionals to gain tailored insights. This book is your resource; revisit it as you navigate your path to retirement. Embrace the strategies we've discussed. Feel empowered and confident in your ability to apply this knowledge.

Retirement is not just about financial security; it's an opportunity for growth and fulfillment. Embrace a holistic approach prioritizing health, continuous learning, and social connections. This stage of life is a chance to explore passions and deepen relationships, enriching your experience beyond financial goals.

I am grateful for choosing this book as a companion on your journey. Your commitment to understanding and securing your financial future is commendable. I'm confident in your ability to achieve fiscal independence and a secure retirement. Let this book be a stepping stone, not the final destination.

Your journey doesn't end here. Continue to seek additional resources and join communities of like-minded individuals. Stay informed about financial trends and share your insights with others. Your experiences can inspire and empower those around you, fostering a community of financially savvy individuals.

Remember that retirement planning is more than a checklist—it's a transformative opportunity. Shift your perspective from viewing it as a source of anxiety to embracing it as an exciting chapter of personal and financial growth. With preparation and a willingness to learn, you hold the power to create a retirement filled with purpose and joy.

REFERENCES

1. **6 Financial Advising Trends for 2023.** (n.d.). *US News Money.* Retrieved from https://money.usnews.com/financial-advisors/articles/financial-advising-trends-this-year

2. **401(k) audit requirements: Everything you need to know.** (n.d.). *BPM.* Retrieved from https://www.bpm.com/insights/401k-audit-requirements-everything-you-need-to-know/

3. **The Best Personal Finance and Budgeting Apps for 2024.** (n.d.). *PCMag.* Retrieved from https://www.pcmag.com/picks/the-best-personal-finance-services

4. **Effective debt management: Tips and strategies.** (n.d.). *Ameriprise.* Retrieved from https://www.ameriprise.com/financial-goals-priorities/personal-finance/effective-debt-management

5. **How to Invest at Every Age.** (n.d.). *Investopedia.* Retrieved from https://www.investopedia.com/articles/investing/090915/are-your-investments-right-your-age.asp

6. **Choosing IRA Accounts: The Best Guide for Beginners.** (n.d.). *Investopedia.* Retrieved from https://www.investopedia.com/articles/personal-finance/032715/best-ira-accounts-beginners.asp

7. **9 Asset Classes for Protection Against Inflation.** (n.d.). *Investopedia.* Retrieved from https://www.investopedia.com/articles/investing/081315/9-top-assets-protection-against-inflation.asp

8. **Utilization and Price Drivers of Increasing Health Care.** (n.d.). *Altarum.* Retrieved from https://altarum.org/news-and-insights/utilization-and-price-drivers-increasing-health-care-spending-2010-2023

9. **Health Insurance Marketplace Calculator.** (n.d.). *KFF.* Retrieved from https://www.kff.org/interactive/subsidy-calculator/

10. **Taxpayers should review the 401(k) and IRA limit increases.** (n.d.). *Internal Revenue Service.* Retrieved from https://www.irs.gov/newsroom/taxpayers-should-review-the-401k-and-ira-limit-increases-for-2023#:~=The%20amount%20individuals%20can%20contribute,also%20all%20increase%20for%202023.

11. **Make the Most of a Roth Conversion With These Strategies.** (n.d.). *SmartAsset.* Retrieved from https://smartasset.com/retirement/schwab-roth-conversion-strategies

12. **Tax-Smart Strategies for Account Withdrawals.** (n.d.). *Kiplinger.* Retrieved from https://www.kiplinger.com/taxes/taxes/tax-smart-strategies-for-account-withdrawals

13. **Income Taxes and Your Social Security Benefit.** (n.d.). *Social Security Administration.* Retrieved from https://www-origin.ssa.gov/benefits/retirement/planner/taxes.html

14. **What Is the Average Retirement Savings in the U.S.?** (n.d.). *The Motley Fool.* Retrieved from https://www.fool.com/research/average-retirement-savings/

15. **How Inflation Impacts Your Retirement Income.** (n.d.). *Investopedia.* Retrieved from

https://www.investopedia.com/articles/retirement/052616/how-inflation-eats-away-your-retirement.asp#:~=The%20inflation%20rate%20affects%20how,financial%20plan%20for%20the%20future.

16. **Early Retirement: The Pros and (Mostly) Cons.** (n.d.). *Investopedia.* Retrieved from https://www.investopedia.com/articles/personal-finance/073114/pros-and-mostly-cons-early-retirement.asp

17. **Benefits Planner: Retirement | Delayed Retirement Credits.** (n.d.). *Social Security Administration.* Retrieved from https://www.ssa.gov/benefits/retirement/planner/delayret.html

18. **Retirement Income Strategies for the Long Haul.** (n.d.). *Kiplinger.* Retrieved from https://www.kiplinger.com/retirement/retirement-income-strategies-for-the-long-haul

19. **Annuities Are Offering Richer Payouts. Here Are the 100 Best Annuities.** (n.d.). *Barron's.* Retrieved from https://www.barrons.com/articles/best-annuities-retirement-income-interest-rates-payouts-f0df855c

20. **Pension Maximization: What it Means, How it Works.** (n.d.). *Investopedia.* Retrieved from https://www.investopedia.com/terms/p/pension-maximization.asp

21. **Planning for retirement during market volatility.** (n.d.). *BlackRock.* Retrieved from https://www.blackrock.com/us/individual/education/retirement-volatility-strategies

22. **Living Trust vs. Will: Key Differences.** (n.d.). *National Council on Aging.* Retrieved from https://www.ncoa.org/adviser/estate-planning/living-trust-vs-will/#:~=some%20significant%20differences.-,A%20will%20is%20a%20simple%20legal%20document%20that%20provides%20instructions,time%20determined%20by%20the%20creator

23. **Estate Planning Mistakes & How To Avoid Them.** (n.d.). *Trust & Will.* Retrieved from https://trustandwill.com/learn/estate-planning-mistakes

24. **Creating A Legacy That Matters.** (n.d.). *Chief Executive.* Retrieved from https://chiefexecutive.net/creating-a-legacy-that-matters/

25. **How To Balance Retirement Security With Philanthropic Goals.** (n.d.). *First Business Bank.* Retrieved from https://firstbusiness.bank/resource-center/how-to-balance-retirement-security-with-philanthropic-goals/#:~=Charities%20will%20never%20pay%20income,will%20offset%20any%20estate%20taxes.

26. **Debunking the Top 6 Financial Myths About Retirement.** (n.d.). *National Council on Aging.* Retrieved from https://www.ncoa.org/article/debunking-the-top-6-financial-myths-about-retirement/

27. **Sustainable withdrawal rates in retirement.** (n.d.). *Vanguard.* Retrieved from https://corporate.vanguard.com/content/dam/corp/research/pdf/sustainable_withdrawal_rates_in_retirement.pdf

28. **How To Protect Retirement Money From Market Volatility.** (n.d.). *Investopedia.* Retrieved from

https://www.investopedia.com/articles/active-trading/121014/protect-retirement-money-market-volatility.asp#:~=When%20markets%20become%20volatile%20as,on%20hand%20should%20also%20grow.

29. **Myths vs. Facts: The state of Social Security.** (n.d.). *Principal Financial Group.* Retrieved from https://www.principal.com/businesses/trends-insights/myths-vs-facts-state-social-security

30. **Physical Activity Benefits for Adults 65 or Older.** (n.d.). *Centers for Disease Control and Prevention (CDC).* Retrieved from https://www.cdc.gov/physical-activity-basics/health-benefits/older-adults.html

31. **Healthy Eating & Meal Planning Tips for Older Adults.** (n.d.). *National Council on Aging.* Retrieved from https://www.ncoa.org/older-adults/health/diet-nutrition/healthy-eating/

32. **11 Meaningful Ways Older Adults Can Volunteer Right Now.** (n.d.). *Forbes.* Retrieved from https://www.forbes.com/health/healthy-aging/volunteer-opportunities-for-older-adults/

33. **Online Classes for Seniors.** (n.d.). *Senior Planet from AARP.* Retrieved from https://seniorplanet.org/classes/

34. **Retirement Planning With Inflation and High Interest Rates.** (n.d.). *Kiplinger.* Retrieved from https://www.kiplinger.com/retirement/retirement-planning-with-inflation-and-high-interest-rates

35. **Case Study: How Financial Planning Helped Secure Their Future.** (n.d.). *LinkedIn.* Retrieved from https://www.linkedin.com/pulse/case-study-how-financial-planning-helped-secure-mark-sweeney

36. **10 Emerging Technologies Shaping the Financial Services Industry.** (n.d.). *Intellias.* Retrieved from https://intellias.com/emerging-technologies-in-financial-services-industry/

37. BiggerPockets. (n.d.). *Real Estate Investing Education.* Retrieved from https://www.biggerpockets.com

38. Kiyosaki, R. T. (1997). *Rich Dad, Poor Dad.* Plata Publishing.

39. U.S. Internal Revenue Service. (n.d.). *Tax Information for Real Estate Investors.* Retrieved from https://www.irs.gov

40. National Association of Realtors. (2023). *Real Estate Market Trends Report.* Retrieved from https://www.nar.realtor

41. Olson, G. (2018). *The Millionaire Real Estate Investor.* McGraw-Hill Education.

42. Schwab, C. (2021). *Guide to Real Estate Crowdfunding.* Retrieved from https://www.schwab.com

43. Graham, B. (2006). *The Intelligent Investor.* Harper Business.

44. Zillow Research. (2023). *Housing Market Insights.* Retrieved from https://www.zillow.com/research

45. U.S. Census Bureau. (2023). *Residential Vacancies and Homeownership Report.* Retrieved from https://www.census.gov

46. Fisher, K. (2015). *Beat the Crowd: How You Can Out-Invest the Herd by Thinking Differently.* Wiley.

Made in United States
Orlando, FL
07 April 2025